Berufsvorbereitung Englisch

Cool!

Lehrerausgabe mit Video-DVD

Herausgeber:
Michael Meisenzahl

Ernst Klett Verlag
Stuttgart · Leipzig

Contents

So arbeiten Sie mit Cool!

Cool! besteht aus sechs Units – und damit Sie sich perfekt zurechtfinden, ist jede davon gleich aufgebaut:

Warm-up

Jede Unit dreht sich um eine Situation, in der Sie Englisch brauchen. Im *Warm-up* steigen Sie mit vielen Bildern, Hör- und Lesetexten in diese Situation ein. Hier wird eine Aufgabe formuliert (*task*), die Sie am Ende der Unit lösen sollen.

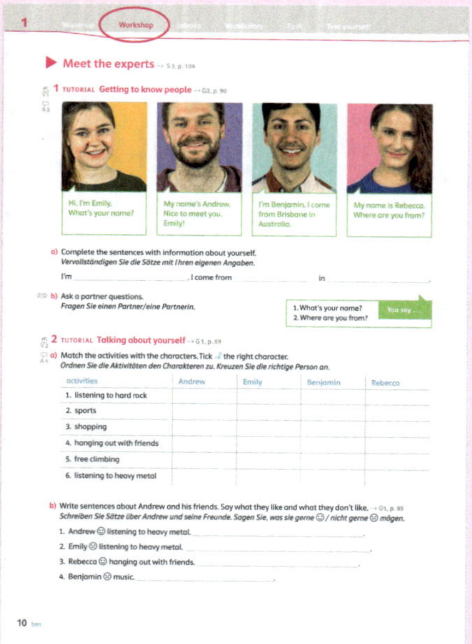

Workshop

Die *task* ist nun bekannt – aber wie löst man sie? Hier kommen Emily, Rebecca, Andrew und Benjamin ins Spiel: Sie zeigen ganz praktisch über Tutorials, wie Sie die Aufgabe problemlos können.

Symbole und Verweise

G 1 Verweis auf die Grammatik im Anhang
○ leichte Übung
● schwere Übung
S 1 Verweis auf Skills im Anhang
A 1 Hörverstehen oder Lesetext zum Anhören
Alle Tracks finden Sie online unter: www.klett.de.
Den Online-Code finden Sie am Anfang jeder Unit.

V1 Video-Tutorials: Alle Videos finden Sie online auf www.klett.de. Den Online-Code finden Sie am Anfang jeder Unit.
Hier arbeiten Sie mit einem Partner/einer Partnerin.
fp3v6k Online-Code: Hier finden Sie alle Hör- und Lesetexte als mp3, die Video-Tutorials sowie das Unit-Vokabular zum Üben.

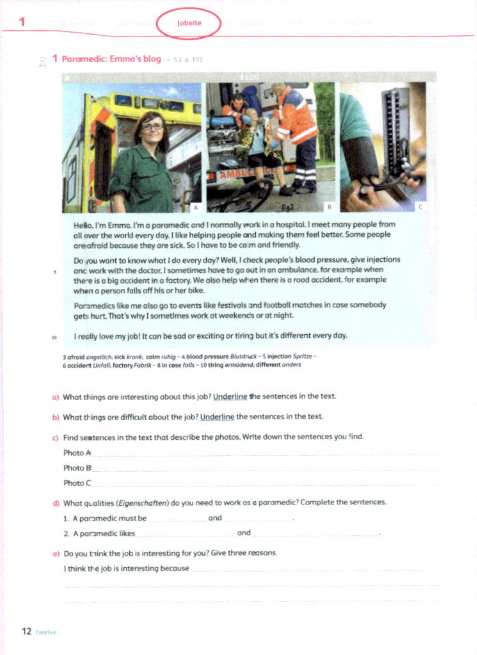

Jobsite

Auf den *Jobsites* werden aktuelle Berufe vorgestellt, die zum Thema der Unit passen und spannende Einblicke in verschiedene Berufsfelder bieten.

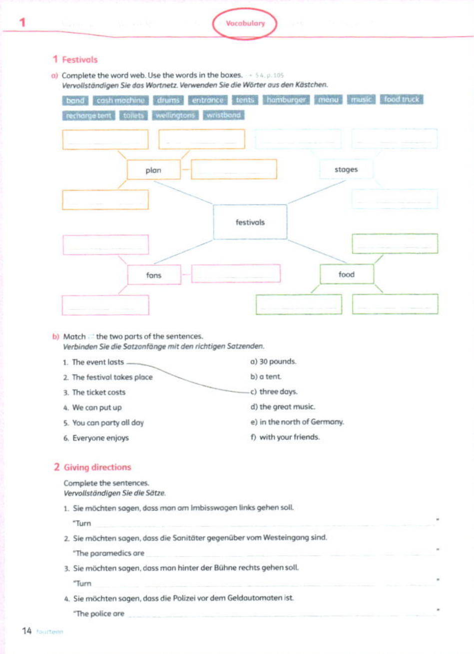

Vocabulary

Hier finden Sie Vokabelübungen zum Wortschatz der Unit.

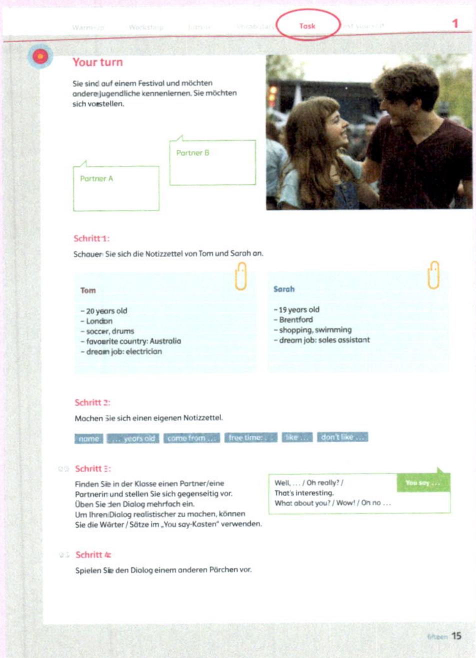

Task

And now it's your turn – jetzt sind Sie dran. Lösen Sie die *task* alleine oder mit einem Partner/einer Partnerin.

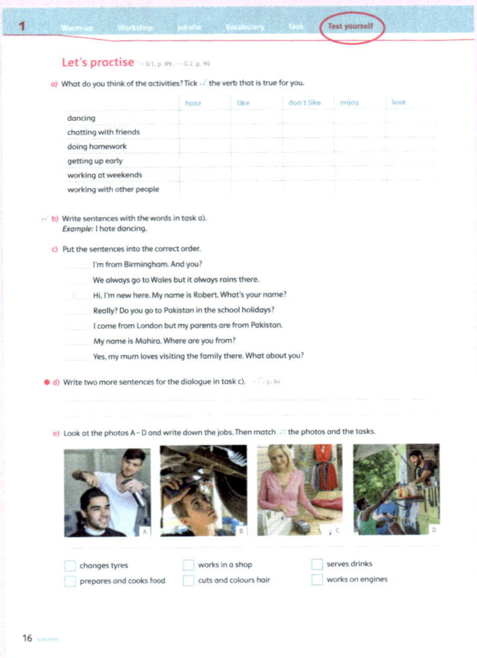

Test yourself

Hier können Sie Ihr Wissen testen. So können Sie sich optimal auf die nächste Prüfung vorbereiten.

1 Making new friends

fp3v6k

A

B

C

D

E

F

1 At a festival

a) Tick ✗ the things you see in the photos.
Kreuzen Sie die Dinge an, die Sie auf den Bildern sehen.

[X] a big stage	[X] a singer	[X] wellingtons	[X] a festival	[ ] great music
[X] fans	[ ] a food truck menu	[X] a camping site	[X] wristbands	[X] mud
[X] hamburgers	[ ] security	[ ] tickets	[X] sunglasses	[X] tents

Am Ende der Unit kann ich ...

- Informationen über Festivals verstehen.
- mich vorstellen.
- neue Leute kennenlernen.

At the end of this unit I can ...

- understand information about festivals.
- introduce myself.
- make new friends.

b) Match ⇄ the words in task a) and the photos.
Ordnen Sie die Begriffe aus Aufgabe a) den Fotos zu.

Photo A *a singer*
Photo B *fans, sunglasses, a festival, wristbands*
Photo C *a camping site, tents*
Photo D *wellingtons, mud*
Photo E *wristbands, a big stage*
Photo F *hamburgers*

c) Choose one photo and describe it. → S 1, p. 102
Wählen Sie ein Foto aus und beschreiben Sie es.

Individuelle Lösung

You say …
I can see a food truck.
There is a stage …
There are many tents …

2 Listening: At the Hurricane festival → S 7, p. 108

A 1

a) Unterstreichen Sie die richtigen Aussagen.

1. Das Hurricane-Festival findet in Süddeutschland / Norddeutschland / Ostdeutschland statt.
2. Das Festival dauert zwei Tage / drei Tage / eine Woche.
3. Es ist ein Heavy-Metal-Festival / Reggae-Festival / Rockfestival.
4. Sie können im Zelt / in der Jugendherberge / bei Gastfamilien übernachten.

b) Complete the sentences. → ◯ p. 84
Vervollständigen Sie die Sätze.

1. The festival lasts *three* days.
2. There are about *100* bands.
3. The tickets cost from *180* to *550* euros.
4. More than *70,000* fans come to see the bands.
5. The cleaners look after *1,700* toilets.

3 Your turn

a) Why are music festivals fun? Why are they not fun? Think of reasons. → G 1, p. 89
Schauen Sie sich die Vor- und Nachteile von Musikfestivals an. Finden Sie weitere Beispiele.

fun	not fun
many young people	*loud*
great music	*too expensive*

b) What do you think of music festivals?
Was denken Sie über Musikfestivals?

I like / don't like music festivals because *Individuelle Lösung*

4 Reading: Amazing facts about festivals → S 2, p. 103

A 2

BLOG

A

B

C

D

Music festivals

The tradition of music festivals is very old. The first music festivals took place 3,000 years ago in Greece. Let's look at some amazing festivals today.

1. The deepest festival is under the sea. It is called the Lower Keys Underwater Festival in Florida. Divers can listen to music and watch tropical fish.
2. The coldest music festival is the Snow Globe Festival in California. On New Year's Eve, you can listen and dance to bands in the snow.
3. The most famous festival in England is probably Glastonbury Festival. Almost 50 years ago, the tickets were only £1 and you even got a glass of fresh milk for free. Glastonbury Festival is great fun but don't forget to bring a good raincoat!

5 **diver** *Taucher/-in;* **tropical** *tropisch* – 6 **New Year's Eve** *Silvester* – 8 **probably** *wahrscheinlich* – 9 **even** *sogar*

a) Match ⇄ the texts 1. – 3. and the pictures. Which picture doesn't match?
Ordnen Sie die Texte 1. – 3. den passenden Bildern zu. Welches Bild passt nicht dazu?

Text 1: B - Text 2: D - Text 3: C

Bild A passt nicht

You say ...
You write £1 but you say "one pound" (*Britisches Pfund*).

b) Tick ✗ the correct box: true or false?
Kreuzen Sie das richtige Kästchen an: richtig oder falsch?

	true	false
1. The first music festivals in history were in Canada.	☐	X
2. The Lower Keys Festival is under the sea.	X	☐
3. You can go to the Snow Globe Festival in California after Christmas.	X	☐
4. Fans get a raincoat for free with the ticket to Glastonbury Festival.	☐	X

c) Beantworten Sie die Fragen.

1. Wann fanden die ersten Musikfestivals statt? Vor 3.000 Jahren.
2. Auf welchem Festival wird man auf jeden Fall nass? Glastonbury Festival.
3. Was gab es früher beim Glastonbury Festival umsonst? Ein Glas Milch.

5 Getting around a festival

a) Match ⇄ the signs with the words.
Ordnen Sie die Piktogramme den richtigen Begriffen zu.

cash machine | toilets | police | food truck | recharge tent | paramedics | information

1. *paramedics*
2. *information*
3. *toilets*
4. *food truck*
5. *recharge tent*
6. *cash machine*
7. *police*

b) You are working at the information at a music festival. Answer the questions.
Sie arbeiten an der Information eines Musikfestivals. Beantworten Sie die Fragen.

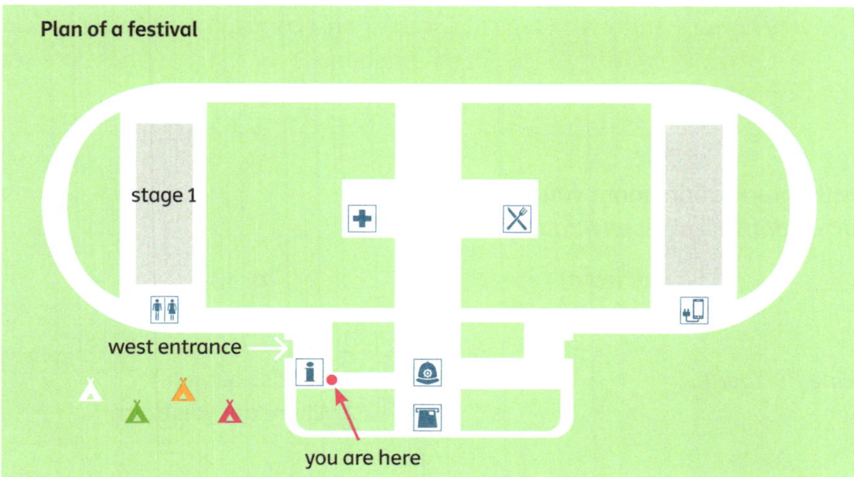

You say ...

- turn left ←
- turn right →
- walk straight on ↑
- next to
- opposite → ←
- behind
- in front of

1. "Excuse me, where are the toilets?"

   You: *Turn left here and walk straight on. The toilets are in front of you.*

2. "I need some cash. Is there a cash machine near here?"

   You: *Yes, walk straight on. Then turn right at the police tent.*

3. "I've hurt my leg. Can you tell me the way to the paramedics, please?"

   You: *Of course. Walk straight on and turn left at the police tent. The paramedics are opposite stage 1.*

4. "My smartphone is dead. Can you help me?"

   You: *Sure. Walk straight on, then turn left at the east entrance. Turn right and the recharge tent is in front of you.*

c) Choose one of the scenes in task b) and act it out with a partner. **OR** ● Think of another situation at the information with your partner. Write a scene and act it.

Your task

Jugendliche aus aller Welt treffen sich auf einem Festival. Die gemeinsame Sprache ist Englisch.

Sie möchten andere Jugendliche kennenlernen. Kein Problem!
Rebecca, Andrew, Benjamin und Emily zeigen Ihnen, wie man das auf Englisch macht.

▶ Meet the experts → S 3, p. 104

1 TUTORIAL Getting to know people → G2, p. 90

V1 A3

Hi, I'm Emily.
What's your name?

My name's Andrew.
Nice to meet you, Emily!

I'm Benjamin. I come from Brisbane in Australia.

My name is Rebecca.
Where are you from?

a) Complete the sentences with information about yourself.
Vervollständigen Sie die Sätze mit Ihren eigenen Angaben.

I'm ______________________. I come from ________________ in ____________________.

b) Ask a partner questions.
Fragen Sie einen Partner/eine Partnerin.

You say ...
1. What's your name?
2. Where are you from?

2 TUTORIAL Talking about yourself → G 1, p. 89

V2 A4

a) Match the activities with the characters. Tick ✗ the right character.
Ordnen Sie die Aktivitäten den Charakteren zu. Kreuzen Sie die richtige Person an.

activities	Andrew	Emily	Benjamin	Rebecca
1. listening to hard rock		X		
2. sports			X	
3. shopping		X		X
4. hanging out with friends				X
5. free climbing			X	
6. listening to heavy metal	X			

b) Write sentences about Andrew and his friends. Say what they like and what they don't like. → G1, p. 89
Schreiben Sie Sätze über Andrew und seine Freunde. Sagen Sie, was sie gerne ☺ / nicht gerne ☹ mögen.

1. Andrew ☺ listening to heavy metal. Andrew likes listening to heavy metal.
2. Emily ☹ listening to heavy metal. Emily doesn't like listening to heavy metal.
3. Rebecca ☺ hanging out with friends. Rebecca likes hanging out with friends.
4. Benjamin ☹ music. Benjamin doesn't like music.

V3 A5

3 TUTORIAL Talking about jobs

a) Which jobs does Emily talk about? Tick the boxes.
Über welche Jobs spricht Emily? Kreuzen Sie die richtigen Kästchen an.

[X] car mechanic

[X] shop assistant

[X] hairdresser

[ ] caterer

[ ] personal assistant

[ ] security

[X] waitress/waiter

[X] electrician

b) What does Emily say about the following jobs? Tick the correct answer.
Was sagt Emily über die folgenden Jobs? Kreuzen Sie die richtige Antwort an.

1. A car mechanic …
   - [X] repairs engines.
   - [ ] checks broken parts.
   - [ ] likes working with people.

2. A hairdresser's main tasks are …
   - [ ] chatting to other hairdressers.
   - [X] cutting hair.
   - [ ] making coffee.

3. An electrician …
   - [ ] repairs engines.
   - [X] works in people's homes.
   - [ ] chats to customers.

4. A waiter's main tasks are …
   - [X] taking orders.
   - [ ] cleaning the kitchen.
   - [ ] meeting people.

c) Choose one of the jobs in exercise b). Tell a partner three things you do in that job. → p. 84
Wählen Sie einen der Jobs in Aufgabe b). Nennen Sie einem Partner/einer Partnerin drei Dinge, die man in diesem Job tut.

Individuelle Lösung

1 Paramedic: Emma's blog → S 2, p. 103

A 6

BLOG

A

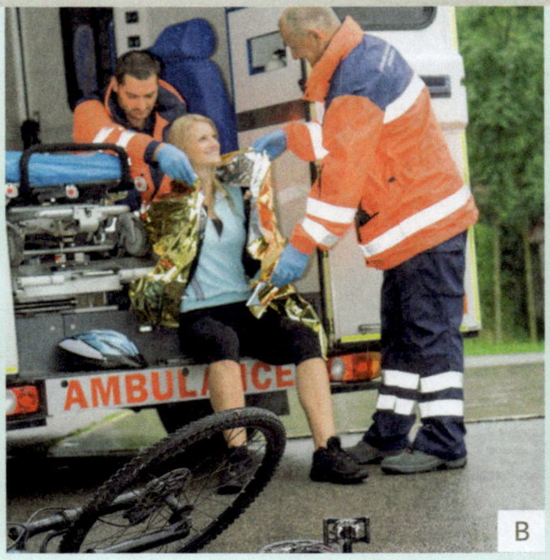

B

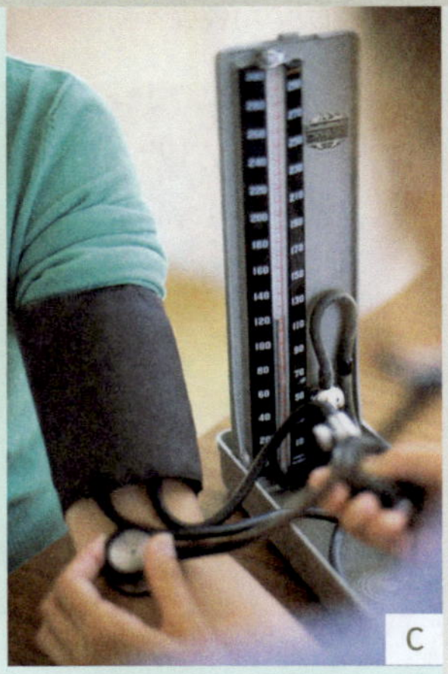
C

Hello, I'm Emma. I'm a paramedic and I normally work in a hospital. I meet many people from all over the world every day. I like helping people and making them feel better. Some people are afraid because they are sick. So I have to be calm and friendly.

Do you want to know what I do every day? Well, I check people's blood pressure, give injections and work with the doctor. I sometimes have to go out in an ambulance, for example when there is a big accident in a factory. We also help when there is a road accident, for example when a person falls off his or her bike.

Paramedics like me also go to events like festivals and football matches in case somebody gets hurt. That's why I sometimes work at weekends or at night.

I really love my job! It can be sad or exciting or tiring but it's different every day.

3 **afraid** *ängstlich*; **sick** *krank*; **calm** *ruhig* – 4 **blood pressure** *Blutdruck* – 5 **injection** *Spritze* – 6 **accident** *Unfall*; **factory** *Fabrik* – 8 **in case** *falls* – 10 **tiring** *ermüdend*; **different** *anders*

a) What things are interesting about this job? Underline the sentences in the text.

b) What things are difficult about the job? Underline the sentences in the text.

c) Find sentences in the text that describe the photos. Write down the sentences you find.

Photo A *I sometimes have to go out in an ambulance.*

Photo B *We also help when there is a road accident, for example when a person falls off his or her bike.*

Photo C *I check people's blood pressure.*

d) What qualities (*Eigenschaften*) do you need to work as a paramedic? Complete the sentences.

1. A paramedic must be *calm* and *friendly*.
2. A paramedic likes *helping people* and *making them feel better*.

e) Do you think the job is interesting for you? Give three reasons.

I think the job is interesting because *Individuelle Lösung*

2 Caterer: Looking for help

A7

The Food Truck is looking for help for the summer.

Do you like meeting people at festivals and sports events?
Do you enjoy working in a small team?
Do you like doing different tasks every day?
Do you hate wearing a uniform?
Do you like travelling?

Then **The Food Truck** wants to hear from you.

We cook and serve Asian and Irish food all over Ireland.
The working hours are from 11 a.m. to 9 p.m.
The day starts at the vegetable market.
Cooking begins at 12 o' clock.
We have to clean the truck by 9 p.m.

Interested?
Then contact Charlie from **The Food Truck** at food@truck.

serving food

cooking

cleaning

taking money

8 to enjoy *genießen* – **13 to serve** *servieren*; **Asian** *asiatisch*

a) Present the job in the food truck to a partner.
Example: You start work at 11 o' clock.

b) Is the job interesting for you or not? Find reasons in the text and write them down.

meeting people at festivals
working in a small team
doing different tasks every day
hate wearing a uniform
travelling

c) Tell a partner why the job is interesting or not.
Example: You do different tasks every day.

You say ...
I like the job because ...
I don't like the job because ...

Individuelle Lösung

1 Festivals

a) Complete the word web. Use the words in the boxes. → S 4, p. 105
Vervollständigen Sie das Wortnetz. Verwenden Sie die Wörter aus den Kästchen.

band | cash machine | drums | entrance | tents | hamburger | menu | music | food truck | recharge tent | toilets | wellingtons | wristband

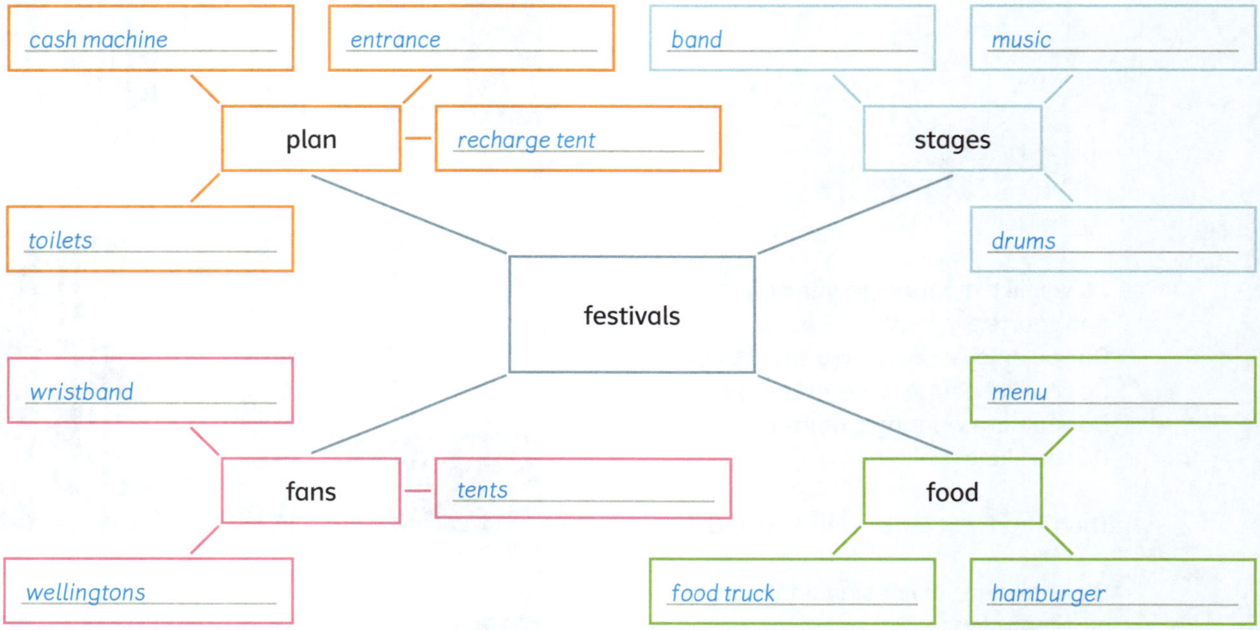

b) Match ⇄ the two parts of the sentences.
Verbinden Sie die Satzanfänge mit den richtigen Satzenden.

1. The event lasts
2. The festival takes place
3. The ticket costs
4. We can put up
5. You can party all day
6. Everyone enjoys

a) 30 pounds.
b) a tent.
c) three days.
d) the great music.
e) in the north of Germany.
f) with your friends.

2 Giving directions

Complete the sentences.
Vervollständigen Sie die Sätze.

1. Sie möchten sagen, dass man am Imbisswagen links gehen soll.
   "Turn left at the food truck."
2. Sie möchten sagen, dass die Sanitäter gegenüber vom Westeingang sind.
   "The paramedics are opposite the west entrance."
3. Sie möchten sagen, dass man hinter der Bühne rechts gehen soll.
   "Turn right behind the stage."
4. Sie möchten sagen, dass die Polizei vor dem Geldautomaten ist.
   "The police are in front of the cash machine."

Your turn

Sie sind auf einem Festival und möchten andere Jugendliche kennenlernen. Sie möchten sich vorstellen.

Partner A

Partner B

Schritt 1:

Schauen Sie sich die Notizzettel von Tom und Sarah an.

Tom

- 20 years old
- London
- soccer, drums
- favourite country: Australia
- dream job: electrician

Sarah

- 19 years old
- Brentford
- shopping, swimming
- dream job: sales assistant

Schritt 2:

Machen Sie sich einen eigenen Notizzettel.

name | … years old | come from … | free time: … | like … | don't like …

Schritt 3:

Finden Sie in der Klasse einen Partner/eine Partnerin und stellen Sie sich gegenseitig vor. Üben Sie den Dialog mehrfach ein. Um Ihren Dialog realistischer zu machen, können Sie die Wörter / Sätze im „You say-Kasten“ verwenden.

You say …

Well, … / Oh really? / That's interesting. What about you? / Wow! / Oh no …

Schritt 4:

Spielen Sie den Dialog einem anderen Pärchen vor.

Let's practise → G 1, p. 89, → G 2, p. 90

a) What do you think of the activities? Tick ✓ the verb that is true for you.

	hate	like	don't like	enjoy	love
dancing					
chatting with friends					
doing homework					
getting up early					
working at weekends					
working with other people					

b) Write sentences with the words in task a).
Example: I hate dancing.

c) Put the sentences into the correct order.

3 I'm from Birmingham. And you?
7 We always go to Wales but it always rains there.
1 Hi, I'm new here. My name is Robert. What's your name?
5 Really? Do you go to Pakistan in the school holidays?
4 I come from London but my parents are from Pakistan.
2 My name is Mahira. Where are you from?
6 Yes, my mum loves visiting the family there. What about you?

● **d)** Write two more sentences for the dialogue in task c). → ◯ p. 84

Individuelle Lösung

e) Look at the photos A – D and write down the jobs. Then match ⇄ the photos and the tasks.

hairdresser

car mechanic

shop assistant

caterer

- B changes tyres
- D prepares and cooks food
- C works in a shop
- A cuts and colours hair
- D serves drinks
- B works on engines

A 8 **f)** Hören Sie den Text und kreuzen Sie an: richtig oder falsch?

	richtig	falsch
1. Der Besitzer eines Fahrrads soll sich an der Information melden.	☐	☒
2. Das Festival muss wegen schlechten Wetters unterbrochen werden.	☒	☐
3. Der neue Food Truck verkauft Burger.	☒	☐
4. Die After-Hour-Party findet in einer großen Halle statt.	☐	☒
5. Der Campingplatz schließt direkt nach dem letzten Konzert.	☐	☒

owner *Besitzer/-in* – **storm** *Gewitter* – **midnight** *Mitternacht*

A 9 **g)** Read the text and tick the right box: true or false?

The Snow Globe Festival

Think of California in the United States of America and you normally think of sun, sea and sand! But after Christmas many young people put on warm clothes and big boots, and travel to Lake Tahoe in Eastern California. That's where the snow and the music are! The Snow Globe Festival takes place near the lake every year. Many people are on holiday between Christmas and New Year and the festival is a great place to go with friends. Some people bring a tent to sleep in. You can also book a room in a cabin. You can eat and drink and dance and meet young people from all over the world. After all dancing is a very good way to keep warm!

12 **cabin** *Hütte*

	true	false
1. The Snow Globe Festival takes place in Florida.	☐	☒
2. You have to bring warm clothes and boots.	☒	☐
3. There is a river close to the festival.	☐	☒
4. The music festival is in February.	☐	☒
5. You can stay in a cabin.	☒	☐

h) *Sie haben den Text über das Snow Globe Festival gelesen und wollen gerne mit einem Freund hingehen. In einer E-Mail erzählen Sie ihm deshalb davon.*
Schreiben Sie einen zusammenhängenden Text auf Deutsch. Schreiben Sie über folgende Punkte:

- Wo findet das Musikfestival statt?
- Wann ist das Musikfestival?
- Wo kann man übernachten?
- Was kann man dort machen?

Hallo …,
Wie geht es dir? Ich muss dir etwas über ein tolles Musikfestival erzählen.

Musterlösung: Das Snow Globe Musikfestival wird in Kalifornien in den Vereinigten Staaten veranstaltet. Das Festival findet nach Weihnachten statt. Man kann im Zelt oder in einem Zimmer in einer Hütte übernachten. Man kann essen, trinken, tanzen und junge Menschen aus der ganzen Welt kennenlernen. Wollen wir hingehen?

Bis bald,
…

2 Moving out

9u8w2s

1 How do you live?

a) Match ⇄ the living arrangements with the photos. Three arrangements do not match.
Ordnen Sie die Wohnmöglichkeiten den Fotos zu. Drei Möglichkeiten passen nicht.

1. with a boyfriend / girlfriend B
2. in a shared flat E
3. in a house in the country –
4. in a skyscraper C
5. on a houseboat –
6. on your own F
7. in a village –
8. in the city A
9. at home D

Am Ende der Unit kann ich ...

- über meinen Alltag sprechen.
- jemanden nach seinem Tagesablauf fragen.
- mich über Geld unterhalten.

At the end of this unit I can ...

- say what I do / don't do every day.
- ask a partner about his / her day.
- talk about money.

b) Match the statements with the photos.
Ordnen Sie die Aussagen den Fotos zu.

	Photo
1. "I share a flat with other young people. It's cheap and I never feel lonely."	E
2. "I still live at home. It's always lively."	D
3. "I live with my girlfriend – it's nice to spend so much time together."	B
4. "My family and I live in a flat in a quiet street."	A
5. "I live in a flat. I work shifts and I like to be quiet after work."	F
6. "There are 60 flats in the house that I live in."	C

c) Talk about where and how you live.
Sprechen Sie über Ihr Zuhause.

You say ...

I live in a flat.
I don't live in a village, I live in a city.
I live at home ...
I like living in a house because ...
I don't like living in the country because ...

d) Talk to a partner about where you live. Ask and answer the questions. → G 2, p. 90
Tauschen Sie sich mit einem Partner / einer Partnerin über Ihr Zuhause aus. Stellen und beantworten Sie Fragen dazu.

You say ...

You ask ...	You answer ...
Where do you live?	I live in a ... / with...
Do you still live at home?	Yes, because ... / No, I live ...
Do you live in the city?	...
Do you live in a flat?	...

A 10

2 Listening: A room for Jannik → S 7, p. 108

Jannik is starting a job as a car mechanic. His company is in Stuttgart, more than one hour from home. Jannik meets an intern, Patrick, at an orientation day in the company. They talk about where and how they live.

a) *Unterstreichen Sie die richtigen Aussagen.*

1. Patrick kommt aus Spanien / Österreich / Irland.
2. Sheena lebt in einer WG mit zwei Mädchen / einem Jungen / zwei Jungen und einem Mädchen.
3. Jannik wohnt momentan in einer Jugendherberge / bei seinen Eltern / bei seiner Freundin.
4. Jannik kann Patricks Fernseher / Bett / Vorhänge übernehmen.
5. Von der Wohnung zur Arbeit fährt man 5 Minuten / 15 Minuten / 50 Minuten.
6. Jannik schaut sich das Zimmer nächsten Freitag / Anfang März / am Wochenende an.

● **b)** Complete the ad for the room in the shared flat.
Ergänzen Sie die Anzeige zu Janniks zukünftigem Zimmer in der WG.

Room in a shared flat

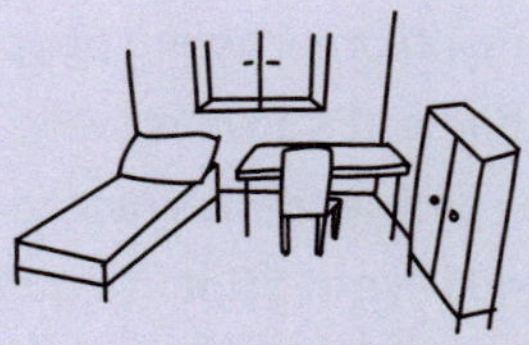

What:	19 m² room in a comfortable flat in Stuttgart
When:	free from April
How much:	rent: € 300, heating and electricity: € 50
Who:	2 flatmates (Paolo and Sofia)
What else:	furnished; there is a bed, a chair, a desk and a wardrobe
Where:	not far from the city centre, near bus stop

Contact Patrick@Stuttgartmail

3 Reading: Three ads → S 2, p. 103

A 11

Studio flat to rent in apartment block, Cork City

Rent: € 450 per month
- living room / bedroom combined
- separate small kitchen
- modern bathroom with shower
- furnished
- high-speed Wi-Fi and an HD TV
- ideal for a single person

Available immediately A

House to rent near Cork City

Rent: € 210 per week
- living room with fireplace
- a country-style kitchen
- 3 bedrooms
- 1 large bathroom, 1 guest toilet
- unfurnished
- a big garden; pets allowed
- bus stop 20 metres from house

Available immediately B

Flat to rent in Fairfield Street, Cork City

Rent: € 550 per month
- living / kitchen area
- 1 bedroom, 1 bathroom with walk-in shower
- fitted kitchen with dishwasher and washing machine
- 5 minutes by car from city centre
- wheelchair access

Available from 1 May 20… C

Ad A: **combined** *in einem Zimmer* – **high-speed** *schnell* – **single person** *Einzelperson* – **available** *bezugsfrei (man kann sofort einziehen)* – Ad B: **fireplace** *Kamin* – **country-style** *im Landstil* – Ad C: **area** *Bereich* – **walk-in shower** *begehbare Dusche* – **fitted kitchen** *Einbauküche* – **wheelchair access** *Eingang für Rollstühle*

Culture Tip
In Germany you ask *„Haben Sie WLAN?“*, in England you ask “Do you have Wi-Fi?”

a) Answer the questions. Write the letters A, B or C.
Beantworten Sie die Fragen. Schreiben Sie die Buchstaben A, B oder C dazu.

Which place	Ad
1. … is not in the city?	B
2. … is furnished?	A
3. … has Wi-Fi?	A
4. … costs the most per month?	B
5. … is not available at the moment?	C

b) Which place is suitable for these people? Fill in the letters A, B or C.
Welche Wohnmöglichkeit passt zu diesen Personen? Schreiben Sie die Buchstaben A, B oder C dazu.

1. Sheena and Patrick: We're looking for a place in or near Cork City. The flat should have a washing machine because we can't afford to buy many things. C
2. Jane: I'm looking for a place in Cork City. I need the flat next month. I don't cook much. A
3. Peter and Corinna Wood: We're a family of four. The children are seven and twelve. We want a place with a garden for our dog. B
4. Jenny: My boyfriend had an accident on his motorbike and he has problems walking. We need a flat that is not far from the city centre. C
5. Tim McMahon: My wife and I want an attractive place in the Cork area. We must sell our house first. There should be a good bus connection to the centre. B

c) Match ⇄ the two parts of the sentences. → G 3, p. 91
Verbinden Sie die Satzanfänge mit den richtigen Satzenden.

You say ...

I can afford a room in a shared flat but I can't afford my own flat.
Jannik has to share the bathroom.
He doesn't have to bring a lot of furniture.
You should look for a place near work.
The flat shouldn't be loud.

1. You have to pay
2. You don't have to bring
3. You can have
4. You have to bring
5. You should like
6. You can't move into

a) a dog or cat in House B.
b) Flat C until May.
c) gardening for House B.
d) your own furniture for House B.
e) € 210 a week for House B.
f) your own furniture for Flat A.

● **d)** Now finish the sentences. Use **can**, **must**, **should** and **don't have to**. → ◯ p. 84, → G 3, p. 91
*Vervollständigen Sie die Sätze. Verwenden Sie **can**, **must**, **should** und **don't have to**.*

1. You must pay € 450 a month for Flat A.
2. You can use a wheelchair in Flat C.
3. You don't have to have a car for House B.
4. House B is unfurnished. You should bring your own furniture.
5. You don't have to drive far to the city from Flat C.

Your task

Jugendliche aus verschiedenen Ländern leben in einer Wohngemeinschaft. Die gemeinsame Sprache ist Englisch. Sie möchten von zuhause ausziehen und sich um ein Zimmer in einer solchen Wohngemeinschaft bewerben. Wie macht man das auf Englisch? Kein Problem – Andrew, Rebecca and Benjamin zeigen Ihnen, wie so etwas abläuft.

Meet the experts

V 4
A 12

1 TUTORIAL Talking about routines → S 3, p. 104

a) What can you see in the photos? Tick the correct statements.
Was sehen Sie auf den Fotos? Kreuzen Sie die richtigen Aussagen an.

A

B

1. Ben is visiting his family. ☐
2. Ben is meeting his new flatmates. ☒
3. Ben is going out to work. ☐
4. Andrew is showing Ben the new sofa. ☐
5. Andrew is cleaning the living room. ☐
6. Andrew is showing Ben the flat. ☒

b) Tick the sentences: true or false?
Kreuzen Sie an: richtig oder falsch?

	true	false
1. Rebecca and Andrew live in a house.	☐	☒
2. Ben helps to look after cars.	☐	☒
3. Rebecca gets up before 7 o'clock.	☐	☒
4. Benjamin sometimes works a night shift.	☒	☐

c) Underline the correct form of the verb. → G2, p. 90
Unterstreichen Sie die richtige Verbform.

1. Andrew: "We want / wants to find out about Benjamin."
2. Benjamin: "I come / comes from Brisbane."
3. Rebecca: "Andrew come / comes from London."
4. Rebecca: "I work / works in a hair salon."
5. Andrew: "Rebecca go / goes into the bathroom at 7."
6. Andrew: "We never get up / gets up before 7."
7. Andrew: "Benjamin want / wants to wash up."

d) Write sentences with the words below. Use the correct form of the verb (come or comes etc) → G 2, p. 90
Bilden Sie Sätze aus den vorgegeben Wörtern. Verwenden Sie die richtige Verbform.

1. (Rebecca / Manchester / come / from) Rebecca comes from Manchester.
2. (work / Andrew / trainee electrician / as/ a) Andrew works as a trainee electrician.
3. (get up / have to / at / Benjamin / 6 o'clock) Benjamin has to get up at 6 o'clock.
4. (on Thursdays / cook / Rebecca and Andrew / always) Rebecca and Andrew always cook on Thursdays.
5. (Benjamin / work / at / sometimes / night) Benjamin sometimes works at night.

e) What do you do every day? Use the phrases in the box.
Was machen Sie jeden Tag? Verwenden Sie die Redemittel im Kästchen.

You say ...
I get up at ...
I go to work / school ...
I come home at ...

f) Complete the sentences. All of them are negative. Use **don't** or **doesn't**. → p. 85
*Vervollständigen Sie die verneinten Sätze. Verwenden Sie **don't** oder **doesn't**.*

cook | cost | know | want | drive

1. A room in a shared flat doesn't cost ___ as much as a house.
2. I don't know ___ much about Australia.
3. Benjamin loves his car but he doesn't drive ___ to work.
4. Rebecca: "I like towns and I don't want ___ to live in the country."
5. Benjamin washes up but he doesn't cook ___.

2 TUTORIAL Talking about housework and money

V 5
A 13

a) When do the young people do the housework? Tick ✓ the correct box.
Wann erledigen die jungen Leute die Hausarbeit? Kreuzen Sie das richtige Kästchen an.

	take out the rubbish	tidy the living room	clean the kitchen	clean the bathroom
Monday	X		X	
Wednesday				X
Friday		X		

b) Look at the photos. Complete the sentences. Use the correct verbs and days from exercise a).
Schauen Sie sich die Fotos an. Vervollständigen Sie die Sätze. Verwenden Sie die richtigen Verben und Tage aus Aufgabe a).

1

2

3

1. Andrew takes out ___ the rubbish on Monday ___.
2. Rebecca cleans ___ the bathroom after work on Wednesday ___.
3. Andrew tidies ___ the living room on Friday ___.

● **c)** *Vervollständigen Sie die Sätze.* → ◯ p. 85

1. Das Zimmer kostet _250_ Pfund im Monat.
2. Wir bezahlen _50_ Pfund für Heizung, Strom und Internet.
3. Jeder gibt _20_ Pfund für Lebensmittel.
4. Benjamin verdient _650 Pfund_ im Monat.

d) Complete the sentences. Use the English words.
Vervollständigen Sie die Sätze. Verwenden Sie die englischen Begriffe.

1. I _often_ ***(oft)*** have to work shifts.
2. I love going to the cinema. I _usually_ ***(gewöhnlich)*** go there on Fridays.
3. I _never_ ***(nie)*** take the train to work. There are too many people on the train.
4. I _sometimes_ ***(manchmal)*** play football with friends after work.
5. Rebecca is a great cook, her food _always_ ***(immer)*** tastes good!

● **e)** Make sentences. Use the words in the boxes. → G2, p. 90
Schreiben Sie vollständige Sätze. Verwenden Sie die Wörter in den Kästchen.

always | often | usually | sometimes | never

1. (get up before … o'clock) _Example: I never get up before …_
2. (take the bus) ______
3. (drink coffee in my break) ______
4. (go shopping) ______
5. (eat in a restaurant) ______

f) Now use your own ideas and make sentences with **always**, **often**, **usually**, **sometimes**, **never**.
Verwenden Sie Ihre eigenen Ideen und bilden Sie Sätze.
Example: *I always take the train to work because it's fast.*

A 14 3 TUTORIAL Asking people what they do

Rebecca and Andrew ask Benjamin to stay for dinner. He wants to find out more about them.

a) Tick ☒ the correct answers.
Kreuzen Sie die richtigen Antworten an.

Benjamin, Andrew and Rebecca talk about …

- [X] the lovely dinner.
- [ ] the housework.
- [X] playing football.
- [X] going to the gym.

b) Listen to the text. Match ⇄ the questions and answers.
Hören Sie sich den Text an. Ordnen Sie die Fragen den Antworten zu.

1. Do you often cook? — c)
2. When do you finish work in the salon? — a)
3. Do you have time for hobbies? — d)
4. How often do you do night shifts? — b)

a) At 8 p.m.
b) Not so often.
c) Yes, usually three times a week.
d) Yes, I do. Cooking is my hobby.

Your turn

Sie möchten von zuhause ausziehen und sich um ein Zimmer in einer internationalen WG bewerben.

A 15

Schritt 1: Schauen Sie sich die beiden Wohnungsanzeigen an und wählen Sie eine davon aus.

SINGLE ROOM NEAR PARK

Our flatmate has moved out and we have a spare room to rent.
The room is in a 3-bedroom flat with a bathroom.
The living room and kitchen are large and comfortable.
The flat is 100 metres from the park so you can go jogging in the summer.
The room is furnished with a bed and a wardrobe.

£350 per month
Available immediately
Contact Paolo, paolo@room2rent

SMALL ROOM TO RENT IN A SUNNY FLAT

The flat has five rooms (one per person).
We are all students.

- Small, sunny, unfurnished room
- No smoking!
- No pets!
- Shared kitchen
- Bathroom with shower

£150 per week
Available from 1 April
Contact Marie-Claire, mcl@room2rent

Schritt 2: Sie wollen sich bei der WG melden. Überlegen Sie sich, was die WG-Bewohner/-innen über Sie wissen möchten. Schauen Sie sich den Notizzettel von Gabriella an. Machen Sie sich nun selbst Notizen.

Name

- I'm a *Individuelle Lösung*
- I have to go to ____________
  from ____________ to ____________.
- I usually come home ____________
- I can help with ____________
- I have ____________
- I don't ____________

Gabriella

- student
- go to college from 8 to 2 in the afternoon
- come home at 4 p.m.
- can help with the washing up, cleaning
- have no pets / have a motorbike
- don't smoke

Schritt 3: Welche Fragen haben Sie an die WG? Hier sind einige Vorschläge: → G2, p. 90

You say ...

You ask...	You answer...
– where / you / come from	We come from ...
– what / you / do	I work in ... / (flatmate's name) goes to ...
– what time / you / get up	We get up at ...
– when / you / come home	We come home at ...
– you / work / at the weekend	We often / never work ...
– how much / you / pay for / heating and electricity	We pay € ...
– you / all cook together	We cook every ...
– what housework / you / have to do	We have to ...

Schritt 4: Finden Sie in der Klasse einen Partner/eine Partnerin. Spielen Sie die Rolle des Bewerbers/der Bewerberin und des WG-Mitglieds. Stellen Sie sich gegenseitig Fragen.

A 16 1 Three jobs in a removals company → S 2, p. 103

Hello, I'm Joe Banks. I want to introduce three people who work in my removals company. Brendan is a mechanic, Fergus is a removals man and Ashling is a trainee office assistant.

My name is Brendan. I help to look after the removal lorries. We repair the lorries when they break down. Every day I have to see if the tyres and lights are OK.
I also check the oil and the brakes. Sometimes the work isn't easy when I have to work under a lorry.
My hands are often greasy and the small tools and parts are difficult to handle.
I also work in the store. My job there is to check that we always have enough parts.
I work five days a week and I also work night shifts. That means I work at night and sleep during the day.
I like my job because it never gets boring. The best thing is that I learn a lot about engines.
One day I'd like to have my own garage.

check the oil

check the brakes

handle tools

Hi, I'm Ashling! I've worked in this office for two years and I have to say it's the right job for me.
What tasks do I do every day? Well, I answer the phone, take messages and arrange appointments for my boss. I also do a lot of photocopying every day.
Last week I organized a meeting for the team. I made coffee and tea for everyone and took notes.
I usually work from Monday to Friday from 9 am to 5 pm. One day I hope to become an office manager.

answer the phone

take notes

8 **to break down** *eine Panne haben*; **tyre** *Reifen* – 9 **brake** *Bremse* – 10 **greasy** *voller Schmieröl*; **tool** *Werkzeug* – 11 **store** *Lager*; **part** *Ersatzteil* – 16 **to take messages** *Nachrichten aufnehmen*; **to arrange appointments** *Termine vereinbaren* – 18 **to take notes** *Notizen machen* – 19 **office manager** *Büroleiter/-in*

drive a removals lorry

My name's Fergus. I'm a removals man. We usually work in a small team. We carry the furniture to the lorry and secure each piece. Then we drive to a new location and unload the furniture. Last week we carried a piano up to the third floor. It was really heavy. We sometimes pack glass or pictures. We have to be very careful with other people's things.
We meet a lot of customers and we always have to be friendly and polite.
We usually work 37 to 42 hours a week. Some of the jobs are at weekends or in the evenings. The salary is about £16,000 a year. I'm going to do my licence next so that I can drive the lorry.

unload boxes

carry furniture to the lorry

21 **to secure** *festmachen* – 22 **to unload** *ausladen* – 23 **floor** *Stockwerk* – 24 **to pack** *einpacken* – 29 **salary** *Gehalt* – 30 **licence** *Führerschein*

a) Choose one job. List the things the person does every day.

b) Tell a partner what the person does every day.
Example: Brendan learns a lot about engines.

c) Look at your list in a). What things are difficult? What things are interesting?

Difficult things	Interesting things
Individuelle Lösung	*Individuelle Lösung*

d) Welche Zukunftspläne haben die drei Angestellten der Firma?

1. Brendan möchte eine eigene Werkstatt eröffnen.

2. Ashling hofft, eines Tages Büroleiterin zu sein.

3. Fergus wird einen LKW-Führerschein machen.

● **e)** Which job (mechanic, office assistant, removals man) do you think is interesting for you? Give your opinion. Write 40 to 50 words in complete English sentences. *(Individuelle Lösung.)*

1 Moving out

a) Complete the word web. Use the words in the box. → S 4, p. 105
Vervollständigen Sie das Wortnetz. Verwenden Sie die Wörter in den Kästchen.

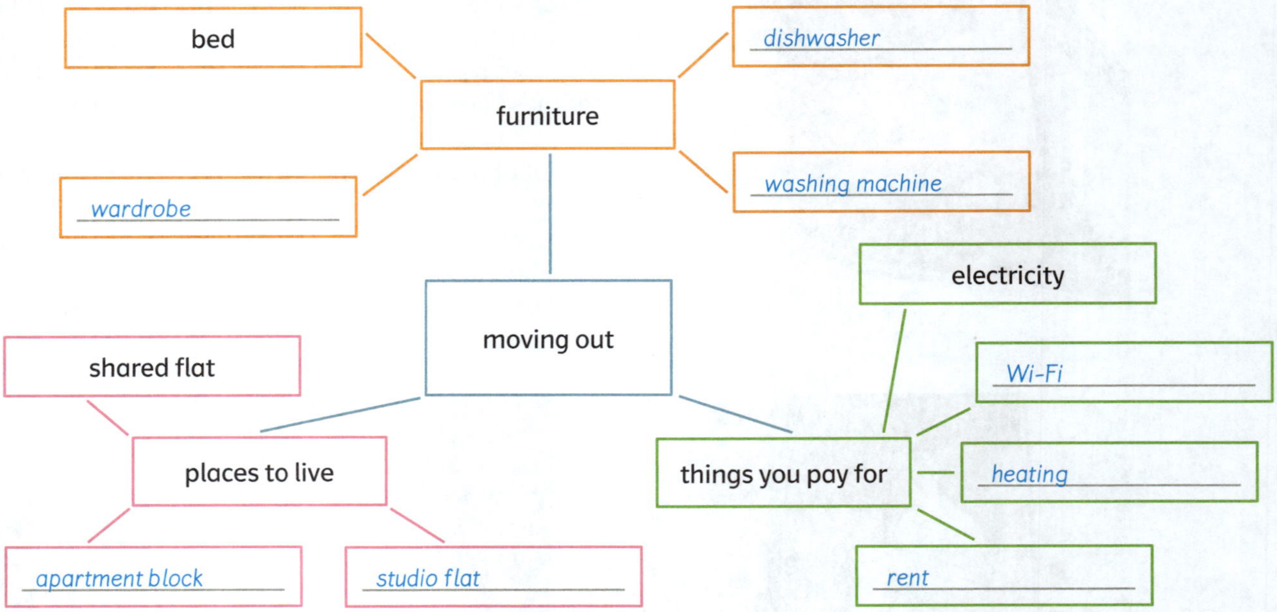

~~shared flat~~ ~~bed~~ ~~electricity~~ washing machine wardrobe dishwasher
Wi-Fi apartment block heating rent studio flat

b) Ask your flatmates for help in the following situations. Match ⇄ the situations with the questions.
Bitten Sie Ihre Mitbewohner in den folgenden Situationen um Hilfe. Ordnen Sie die Situationen den Fragen zu.

Situations	**Questions**
1. The kitchen is very dirty after our cooking night.	a) Can you take out the rubbish?
2. There are papers all over your desk.	b) Can you hoover the living room?
3. My parents are coming to visit.	c) Can you wash up?
4. There is a bad smell *(Geruch)* in the kitchen.	d) Can you tidy it?
5. Look at all of the dirty plates.	e) Can you clean it?

c) Complete Benjamin's message. Use the words in the boxes.
Vervollständigen Sie Benjamins Nachricht. Benutzen Sie die Wörter in den Kästchen.

shared different responsible lovely large private far lively

E-MAIL

Hi Jane,

How are you?
I moved into a shared flat three weeks ago and I like it. The flat is large and has three bedrooms. It is not far from my company. My room is private. I'm responsible for keeping it clean. We all do different jobs in the flat. Every Monday we clean the bathroom. The best thing about the flat are my flatmates. They are very lively. Rebecca usually cooks three times a week. Her dinners are really lovely.
Please write soon.

Benjamin

d) Choose the right beginning and find the verbs.
Wählen Sie den richtigen Wortanfang und bilden Sie Verben.

mo | sha | jo | clo | fe | spe | gu | sou

1. _sha_ re
2. _spe_ nd
3. _sou_ nd
4. _jo_ in
5. _clo_ se
6. _gue_ ss
7. _fe_ el
8. _mo_ ve

2 Talking about routines and money

a) Match ⇄ the two parts of the sentences.
Verbinden Sie die beiden richtigen Satzteile miteinander.

1. I sometimes work shifts
2. I normally start work at 6:30
3. I'm looking for a shared flat that
4. I can't afford
5. If I move in,
6. After work I sometimes go

a) has a good bus connection to my company.
b) I can help with the housework.
c) to the gym.
d) so I have to get up at 5:45.
e) to pay a lot of rent.
f) so I sleep during the day.

b) Complete the sentences about the jobs.
Vervollständigen Sie die Sätze über die Jobs.

1. An _assistant_ takes messages and arranges appointments.
2. A _mechanic_ repairs cars and lorries.
3. A _removals man_ carries heavy furniture.

c) What do these words mean? Tick ✗ the right answer.
Was bedeuten diese Wörter? Kreuzen Sie die richtige Antwort an.

1. on your own
- [ ] with other people
- [ ] with your family
- [x] just you alone

2. to get used to something
- [ ] to have a problem with something
- [x] to be happy with a new situation
- [ ] to change something

3. company
- [ ] a place where people go to eat
- [ ] a place where people live
- [x] a place where people work

A 17

Let's practise → S 2, p. 103, → S 9, p. 110

Floating homes

Like in many countries, it is difficult for young British people to find a place to live when they leave home. Flats and houses are very expensive to rent. Almost 33,000 people in Britain have found a cheaper alternative: They live in houseboats on a waterway.

"Houseboats are becoming a popular alternative to a flat," says Sophia Parry, 19. "I share a boat in the east of London with my boyfriend, Luke."

"That's right. We moved in nine months ago," says Luke.

"The boat is eight feet wide and it's bigger than a room in a shared flat," says Sophia. "There's a bedroom, a small bathroom and toilet, a large living room and a kitchen. And it's furnished."

"Our boat isn't the most wonderful on the water, but we like it," Luke laughs.

Sophia and Luke pay £700 a month in rent and there are the costs for insurance, fuel and electricity.

"Life on a houseboat is nice and relaxed," says Luke who is a carpenter and works in Greenwich.

"But we have to do the same housework that other people do in a flat," says Sophia. "We hoover the rooms every week, clean the bathroom, take out the rubbish and so on. Luke cooks and I clean the kitchen."

"But there's something that's not easy on a houseboat," says Sophia. "Last winter was so cold and the heating isn't good. We had to wear ski suits every night."

1 **floating** *schwimmend* – 7 **waterway** *Wasserstraße* – 8 **popular** *beliebt* – 20 **insurance** *Versicherung* – 20 **fuel** *Treibstoff*

a) *Lesen Sie den Text und entscheiden Sie, ob die Aussagen richtig oder falsch sind.*

	richtig	falsch
1. Der Text handelt von einem Urlaub auf einem Hausboot.	☐	X
2. Sophia und Luke wohnen in einem Hausboot im Osten von London.	X	☐
3. Sophia und Luke haben sich ein Hausboot gekauft.	☐	X
4. Sie haben sich das Hausboot selbst eingerichtet.	☐	X
5. Auf dem Boot fallen weniger Hausarbeiten an.	☐	X
6. Die Heizung auf dem Boot ist nicht besonders gut.	X	☐

● b) *Verbessern Sie die falschen Aussagen.*

1. Der Text handelt von Leuten, die zur Miete auf Hausbooten leben.

3. Sophia und Luke haben das Hausboot gemietet.

4. Das Hausboot war schon möbliert.

5. Sie machen genau dieselbe Hausarbeit wie in einer Wohnung.

c) Finish the sentences with information from the text.

1. Almost 33,000 British people have found an alternative to expensive _flats_.
2. Luke's and Sophia's houseboat is in _the east of London_.
3. The houseboat has a small _bathroom_ and a big _living room_.
4. A big problem with the houseboat is the _heating_.

d) What are the pros and cons of a houseboat? Could you imagine living on a houseboat? Say why or why not. Write 40 to 50 words in complete English sentences.

Individuelle Lösung

A 18 e) *Sophia und Luke besuchen ein Paar auf einem anderen Hausboot. Sie hören nun das Gespräch. Kreuzen Sie die richtige Lösung an.*

1. Sophia und Luke bringen ein Geschenk mit:

☐ eine Flasche Wein ☐ ein Buch über London ☒ einen Blumenstrauß

2. Sophia arbeitet als Auszubildende in …

☒ einem Blumenladen ☐ einer Werkstatt ☐ einem Krankenhaus

3. Luke baut …

☐ Boote ☒ Möbel ☐ Häuser

f) *Sie rufen in einer internationalen WG wegen eines Zimmers an. Die Ansprechpartnerin in der WG heißt Judy. Was würden Sie im Dialog auf Englisch sagen?*

Judy: Hello.

You: Hier spricht … Ich habe deine Anzeige im Internet gesehen. Ist das Zimmer noch frei?

My name is … I saw your ad on the Internet. Is the room still available?

Judy: Yes it is.

You: Wie hoch ist die monatliche Miete?

How much is the rent per month?

Judy: The rent for the room is 250 euros per month.

You: Ok. Was muss ich in der WG alles machen?

What housework do I have to do in the shared flat?

Judy: We all have to clean the kitchen and bathroom and wash the dishes.

You: Meinst du, dass ich das Zimmer anschauen kann?

Do you think that I can look at the room?

Judy: Yes. Can you come tomorrow at half past four?

You: Ja, vielen Dank. Bis morgen um halb fünf.

Yes, thank you. See you tomorrow at half past four.

3 Travelling on a budget

🌐 gg7v6s

A

B

C

E

D

F

G

1 Let's go on a trip!

a) Tick ×✓ the things you see in the photos.
Kreuzen Sie an, was Sie auf den Fotos sehen.

- [X] the world
- [X] a plane
- [X] a couch
- [X] an au pair
- [X] farmwork
- [X] a hostel
- [ ] sights
- [X] a backpack
- [X] a kangaroo
- [ ] a ship

Am Ende der Unit kann ich ...
- Informationen über günstige Reisemöglichkeiten verstehen.
- eine Übernachtungsmöglichkeit organisieren.
- meine Familie und Herkunft beschreiben.

At the end of this unit I can ...
- understand information about cheap travel options.
- arrange an overnight stay.
- describe my family and background.

b) Match ⇄ the words in a) with the photos.
Ordnen Sie die Wörter aus Aufgabe a) den passenden Fotos zu.

Photo A: *the world*

Photo B: *a couch, a backpack*

Photo C: *a plane*

Photo D: *an au pair*

Photo E: *a hostel, a backpack*

Photo F: *farmwork*

Photo G: *a kangaroo*

A 19

2 Listening: Cheap travel options → S 7, p. 108

You want to see the world but you don't have much money? Then maybe working in a foreign country is perfect for you! Let's listen to three people who spent some time abroad.

a) Listen to the text. Who did what? Tick the correct answer.
Hören Sie sich die Texte an. Wer hat was gemacht? Kreuzen Sie die richtige Antwort an.

	farmwork	Au-Pair	visit family	couchsurfing
Lisa		X		
Jake	X			
Hannah				X

b) *Complete the sentences. Use the correct form of the verb.* → G 4, p. 93
Vervollständigen Sie die Sätze. Verwenden Sie die richtige Form des Verbs.

1. Last year Lisa *worked* (to work) as an au pair in Canada.
2. She always *had* (to have) time to visit some sights at the weekends.
3. Jake *travelled* (to travel) around Australia for some time.
4. He *didn't need* (not need) much money for hostels.
5. Hannah's hosts *showed* (to show) her lots of interesting places.
6. They let her sleep on a couch so she *didn't have* (not have) to pay.

> **You say ...**
> I lived with a host family.
> We didn't go to the farm yesterday.
> She brought the children to school.

c) Complete the sentences. → p. 85
Vervollständigen Sie die Sätze.

1. An au pair takes care of the *children* of a family.
2. If you want to work as an au pair you need to have some experience as a *babysitter*.
3. If you want to work on a farm you don't need money for a *hostel*.
4. You need to be fit and like working *outside*.
5. Your hosts will let you sleep on their *couch*.
6. You can travel like Hannah if you like meeting new *people*.

d) Complete the table with the following words.
Vervollständigen Sie die Tabelle mit den folgenden Wörtern.

farm | bring children to school | play | milk cows | fit | sofa | patient | host family | pick apples | friendly | work outside | get to know hosts | make breakfast | get to know cities | change tyres | open-minded

	Where you live	What you need to be	What you do
	host family	patient, friendly	bring children to school, play, make breakfast
	farm	fit	milk cows, pick apples, change tyres, work outside
	sofa	open-minded	get to know hosts, get to know cities

e) Look at the offers and make comparisons. → G 5, p. 94 → ◯ p. 85
Schauen Sie sich die Angebote an und machen Sie Vergleiche.

Example: The working hours in Position A are longer than in Position B.

	Position A	Position B
working hours per week	30	25
number of months	10 months	12 months
salary per week	$ 100	$ 120
host family	4 people	4 people
cost of flight	$ 970	$ 865

You say …

I am two years older than you.
Ben is more patient than Emily.
I am as old as my friend Tom.

3 Your turn

Which travel option do you find interesting? Explain why. You can use a dictionary to look up unfamiliar words. → S 5, p. 106
Welche Reisemöglichkeit finden Sie interessant? Erklären Sie, warum. Sie können ein Wörterbuch verwenden, um unbekannte Wörter nachzuschlagen.

Example: I would like to work on a farm because I like being outside and I love animals.

Individuelle Lösung

A 20

4 Reading: How to use rent-a-couch → S 2, p. 103

BLOG

Step 1:
Create your rent-a-couch profile: say who you are, how old you are and where you are from. It's also helpful to say something about your hobbies and what you would like to see and do in the city. Maybe you can find a host who has the same interests.

Step 2:
Use the search engine on rent-a-couch to find the perfect host for you: type in your arrival and departure dates and the city you want to visit.

Step 3:
Filter your search results: you can look at a map to see where the hosts live or you can filter your results by different categories (single hosts, families, pet-friendly hosts etc.).

Step 4:
Contact your host: pick a place you like and fill in the form to contact your host. He or she can look at your profile and send you an email as quickly as possible.

2 **to create** *erstellen* – 6 **search engine** *Suchmaschine* – 6 **arrival** *Ankunft* – 7 **departure** *Abreise* – 9 **to filter** *filtern / sortieren* – 10 **pet-friendly** *tierfreundlich*

a) Tick ×✓ the correct box: true or false?
Kreuzen Sie das richtige Kästchen an: richtig oder falsch?

	true	false
1. You have to include your address in your profile.	☐	X
2. You have to type in your arrival and departure dates.	X	☐
3. You can't filter your search results.	☐	X
4. You can also find pet-friendly hosts.	X	☐
5. You can contact your host with an online form.	X	☐
6. Your host will phone you.	☐	X

b) *Beantworten Sie die Fragen (Stichworte genügen).*

1. Welche Informationen über sich selbst sollen Sie auf Ihrem Profil hinterlegen?
   Name, Alter, Wohnort, ggf. Hobbys und Pläne
2. Welche Daten müssen Sie in die Suchmaschine eingeben? *An- und Abreise*
3. Wie können Sie die Suchergebnisse filtern? *z.B. Single-Gastgeber, Familien, tierfreundliche Gastgeber*
4. Wie können Sie Kontakt aufnehmen zu den Gastgebern? *Online-Formular*
5. Wie wird sich Ihr Gastgeber bei Ihnen melden? *per E-Mail*

Your task

Sie möchten verreisen und auf rent-a-couch einen Gastgeber finden, Kontakt mit ihm aufnehmen und sich auf das erste Telefonat mit ihm vorbereiten.

Meet the experts

1 TUTORIAL Finding a place to stay → S 3, p. 104

V 6
A 21

a) Watch the tutorial and fill in the online form for Andrew.
Schauen Sie das Tutorial an und füllen Sie das Online-Formular für Andrew aus.

ONLINE FORM

Name:	*Andrew Young*
Destination:	*Dublin*
Arrival:	*10 April*
Departure:	*13 April*
No. of people travelling:	*1*
Plans:	*see sights, go to events*

You say ...
You say: the first of March
You write: 1 March

b) Complete the online form. Use the correct form of the verbs. → G 6, p. 95
Vervollständigen Sie das Online-Formular. Verwenden Sie die richtigen Verbformen.

to look | to travel | to look forward to | to plan | to start

Hi, my name is Andrew. I *am looking* for a place to stay in Dublin. I *am planning* to stay for three nights. My trip *is starting* on 10 February. I am from Dallas in the US but I *am travelling* across Europe right now. It would be great if I could have somewhere to stay in Dublin. I don't know Dublin but I *am looking forward to* getting to know the sights and the people. I will be easy to live with and maybe you can show me some interesting places.

c) Look at the offers from hosts in Dublin. Decide which offer Andrew would choose and say why.
Schauen Sie sich die Angebote von Gastgebern in Dublin an. Entscheiden Sie, welches Angebot Andrew auswählen würde und begründen Sie Ihre Entscheidung.

INTERNET

Sean
Hey traveller, welcome to Dublin. I'm a great guy and I can show you the best places in town. I live in Blackrock which is just a 10-minute train trip from the city centre. Or I can lend you a bike when you're here.

Nawid
Hello Andrew. I can offer you a couch in my apartment if you are a quiet and undemanding guest. I prefer travellers who are over 30 years old. I live with my wife and three children near the city centre.

Mary
Welcome to Dublin, the greatest city in the world :-) I work as a tourist guide and my flat is close to the city centre. I live with my small daughter and my cat. They both love visitors. Hope to meet you soon, Andrew!"

2 **guy** *Typ* – 5 **to lend** *ausleihen* – 8 **undemanding** *anspruchslos* – 8 **to prefer** *bevorzugen* – 13 **flat** *Wohnung*

I think Andrew would choose *Individuelle Lösung* ____________ because ____________.

2 TUTORIAL How to talk on the phone

A 22

a) Listen to the phone call and fill in the correct information. → ◯ p. 86
Hören Sie sich das Telefonat an und tragen Sie die richtigen Informationen ein.

You say ...
My name is ...
I'm calling about ...
Can I speak to ..., please?
Sorry, can you repeat that, please?
Sorry, I didn't understand you.

1. Name of host: *Mary*
2. Date of Andrew's visit: *10 to 13 of April*
3. Time of arrival: *5 p.m.*
4. Bus numbers: *747 and 51*
5. Street name: *McHenry Street*
6. Flat number: *34 A*

b) Match ⇄ the parts of the sentences.
Verbinden Sie die richtigen Satzhälften miteinander.

1. Hello, this is
2. Can I speak to
3. What can I do
4. I am calling about
5. Can you recommend
6. How do I get to
7. I'm looking forward to
8. See you

a) soon. Take care.
b) meeting you.
c) any interesting events?
d) Andrew.
e) your offer of a couch.
f) for you?
g) Mary, please?
h) your place?

c) Choose the correct answer.
Wählen Sie die richtige Antwort.

I can offer you my couch | I live just outside of town | See you soon then! | A great band is playing in the pub tonight | Welcome to Dublin, Andrew!

1. "I will visit you next month." – *See you soon then!*
2. "Nice to meet you, Mary!" – *Welcome to Dublin, Andrew!*
3. "Can you recommend any events?" – *A great band is playing in the pub tonight.*
4. "I'm looking for a place to stay in June" – *I can offer you my couch.*
5. "Do you live in the city centre?" – *I live just outside of town.*

d) Work with a partner and do a little role play. One of you is the guest, the other the host. Use the information on the role cards and act out the telephone conversation. → S 6, p. 107
Arbeiten Sie mit einem Partner/einer Partnerin und machen Sie ein kleines Rollenspiel. Eine/r von Ihnen ist der Gast, der/die andere der Gastgeber. Verwenden Sie die Informationen auf den Rollenkarten und führen Sie ein Telefonat. → Musterlösung Seite 101

Role card HOST:
- Kate Fields
- you can offer a couch in your spare room
- you agree to the dates
- bus no. 12 from the airport to Oxford Street, walk down Oxford Street, your flat is at number 2 Oxford Street
- finish the conversation in a polite and friendly way

Role card GUEST:
- use your own name
- say why you are calling
- tell Kate that you would like to stay from the 8th to 10th March
- ask for directions
- finish the conversation in a polite and friendly way

Write down the questions you want to ask your host.

Is your sofa available from the 8th to 10th March?

How do I get to your apartment?

3 TUTORIAL Meeting your host

V 7

A 23

a) Before you watch the tutorial: match the sentences and the photos. Two sentences don't match.
Bevor Sie sich das Tutorial anschauen: Ordnen Sie die Aussagen den Fotos zu. Zwei Aussagen passen nicht.

1

2

1. "Welcome to Dublin, Andrew!" *photo no. 1*
2. "Can you show me my room please?" *does not match*
3. "Hi, I'm Andrew." *photo no. 1*
4. "Would you like to have another cup of tea?" *photo no. 2*
5. "The kitchen is over there." *does not match*

b) Underline the correct answer.
Unterstreichen Sie die richtige Antwort.

1. Mary has a daughter / a son / two children.
2. Andrew has got an older brother / an older sister / a younger sister.
3. His brother works / lives in Denver / goes to school.
4. Andrew's parents have got a garage / a car salesroom / a shop.
5. Andrew's grandparents look after children / help out in the family business / don't live in Dallas.

c) Fill in the correct form of the verbs. → G 4, p. 93
Tragen Sie die richtige Verbform ein.

After Andrew *finished* (finish) school he *wanted* (want) to see the world. He *went* (go) to Europe and *travelled* (travel) around. He sometimes *slept* (sleep) on people's couches so he *didn't have to* (not have) get a room in a hostel. He *met* (meet) lots of people from all over the world. In the evenings he often *had* (have) dinner with his hosts and *chatted* (chat) with them. They also *showed* (show) him their cities. Sometimes they *had* (have) so much fun together that Andrew *didn't want* (not want) to go home.

d) Work with a partner and do a little role play like Emily and Andrew.

1 WANTED: team member at Dublin City Hostel → S 2, p. 103

A 24

Would you like to work and have fun at the same time? Then we have the perfect job offer for you! Come and be a part of our international team at Dublin City Hostel, right in the heart of the city. We are looking for people to join our team during the summer.

You are the right candidate if you:
- are friendly and energetic
- like meeting new people
- are reliable and take initiative when something needs to be done
- speak fluent English (and ideally another foreign language)

Your tasks include:
- welcoming our guests
- answering any questions they have about our hostel and the city of Dublin
- cleaning rooms
- serving drinks and food in our bar

Experience in hotel work is nice but not required – we offer on-the-job training. Please send your application to manager@dublincity... .ie

2 **a part** *Teil* – 3 **to join** *sich anschließen* – 13 **to serve** *servieren* – 14 **required** *notwendig*; **on-the-job training** *Einarbeitung am Arbeitsplatz*

a) Look at the job advert and find out what qualities you need for the job.

you need to be friendly and energetic

you need to like meeting new people

you need to be reliable and take initiative

you need to speak fluent English and ideally another foreign language

b) Match ⇄ the statements with the photos.

1. "My favourite task is to welcome guests." Photo *A*
2. "In the evenings I often serve drinks in our bar." Photo *C*
3. "Cleaning rooms is boring – but it's part of the job." Photo *B*

c) Do you think the job is interesting for you? Give three reasons.
Example: I think the job is interesting because I like to meet people from all over the world.

Individuelle Lösung

A 25

2 Jacob's blog: Working on a farm

"Hi, I'm Jacob and I work on a farm in the south of England. I finished school last year and I didn't know what I wanted to do. I love nature and animals, so I knew I wanted to do something outside. I didn't want to sit in an office all day long. A friend showed me an advert for a summer job on an organic farm in Germany and I thought this was a great opportunity to see another country and get to know something about organic farming.

In the couple of months I was there I learned a lot. We planted, weeded and watered the crops. I also had to work with farm machines like tractors and mowers. Sometimes I had to change tyres or help to repair broken parts. In the autumn we were very busy picking apples and turning them into organic apple juice and cider. We then sold the products at local farmer's markets and in a little shop on the farm.

The farmers were always friendly and patient with me, and I met some other helpers from all over the world. My experience in Germany helped me to decide to become a farmer. It also helped me to get the job here in England. Although it is hard work, there's nothing like seeing this hard work turn into the most delicious and healthy foods."

4 **office** *Büro* – 6 **organic farm** *Bio-Bauernhof* – 9 **to weed** *Unkraut jäten*; **crops** *das Getreide, die Pflanzen*
10 **mower** *Mähmaschine* – 12 **to repair** *reparieren*; 12 **autumn** *Herbst* – 13 **apple juice** *Apfelsaft* – 18 **delicious** *lecker*

a) Here are some pictures Jacob took on the farm. Find the sentences in the text that describe the pictures.
→ Musterlösung Seite 101

b) Describe what you can see in the pictures. → S 1, p. 102

In the first picture I can see a boy and a girl working on a farm. They are planting crops. I can see many apples in the second picture. I can see a young man driving a tractor in picture number 3. I think he's working on a farm. In the last picture I can see a young man selling fruit and vegetables at a farmers' market.

c) Is the job interesting for you? Write down reasons.

Individuelle Lösung

● **d)** Pick a partner. Tell him/her why the job is interesting or not.

Travelling

a) Complete the text. One word does not fit.
Vervollständigen Sie den Text. Ein Wort passt nicht.

travel | destination | meet new people | hostel | looking forward to | abroad | map | couchsurfing | hosts

Sammy's trip to Ireland

Last year I finished school in July. My job started in September, so I had four weeks off. I had saved some money, it wasn't much but I knew I wanted to go abroad on a holiday. I decided to stay at a hostel in Dublin, Ireland for four nights. Then I wanted to travel around Ireland for ten days. I also wanted to do couchsurfing so that I could save money and meet new people. I was really looking forward to making Irish friends. So I looked at a map of Ireland and decided where I wanted to travel. I contacted couchsurfing hosts and found great people to stay with.

b) Complete the sentences.
Vervollständigen Sie die Sätze.

1. I packed my backpack *(Rucksack)* before my trip to Ireland.
2. My flight *(Flug)* to Dublin landed on time.
3. My host offered me her spare room *(Gästezimmer)* to sleep in.
4. I spent a lot of time exploring the sights *(Sehenswürdigkeiten)* in the city.
5. I saw many famous sights – it was a great experience *(Erfahrung)*.

c) Put the letters into the correct order.
Bringen Sie die Buchstaben in die richtige Reihenfolge.

1. c d e e m m n o r: recommend
2. a a i p r u: au pair
3. a a l r s y: salary
4. d a e r v t: advert
5. a e n r: earn
6. a k s s t: tasks

Qualities

d) Complete the crossword.
Lösen Sie das Kreuzworträtsel.

1. When you don't talk a lot
2. When you like to help people
3. When you do what your boss expects you to do (you are on time, you do your job well etc.)

4. When you are nice to people
5. When you are interested in different people, ideas and opinions
6. When you are sporty and don't get tired quickly
7. When you have a lot of energy
8. When you don't have a problem when you must wait for something or someone
9. When you like to find out things about places and people
10. It's important to know your personal Q U A L I T I E S

							1	Q	U	I	E	T
		2	H	E	L	P	F	U	L			
			3	R	E	L	I	A	B	L	E	
	4	F	R	I	E	N	D	L	Y			
	5	O	P	E	N	-	M	I	N	D	E	D
					6	F	I	T				
7	E	N	E	R	G	E	T	I	C			
			8	P	A	T	I	E	N	T		
	9	I	N	T	E	R	E	S	T	E	D	

Family

e) Look at the family tree and complete the sentences.
Schauen Sie sich den Familien-Stammbaum an und vervollständigen Sie die Sätze.

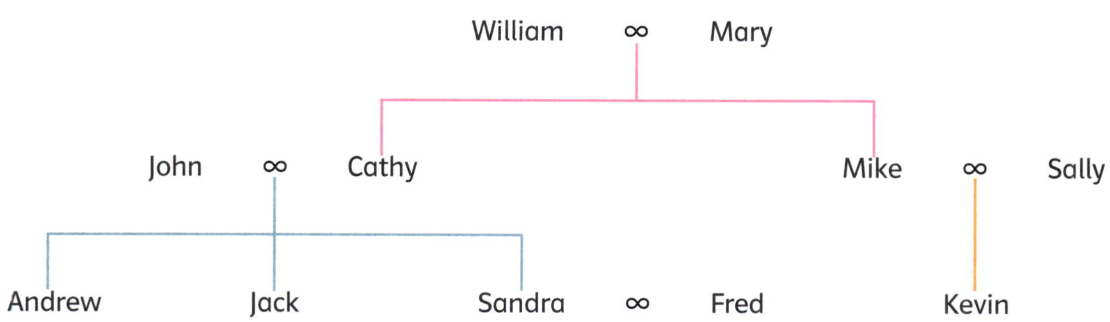

1. William and Mary have two _children_.
2. Andrew is Jack's _brother_ and Sandra is his _sister_.
3. John is Cathy's _husband_.
4. Sandra is Fred's _wife_.
5. Mike and Sally are Kevin's _parents_.

Your turn

Schritt 1: Lesen Sie sich die Anzeigen der Gastgeber auf rent-a-couch durch und wählen Sie einen aus, bei dem Sie gerne übernachten würden.

rent-a-couch

Caro:
Welcome to Stockholm, the greatest city in the world! My husband and I live in a little apartment not far from the city centre. We can tell you a lot about our city, the famous sights, nice restaurants and cool shops!

Dean:
Looking for a place to stay in Manchester? I have a spare room in my apartment just outside of Manchester. Maybe we can visit a football match together when you're here.

Anne & Thomas:
Explore Berlin! We live in a nice flat in Prenzlauer Berg, one of the coolest areas in the city. If you don't mind having two lively children around, our couch is yours – and you can always have a nice cup of coffee in our own café!

I would like to stay with ____________________ because ____.

Schritt 2: Füllen Sie das Online-Formular mit Ihren Angaben aus.

ONLINE FORM

Name:	*Individuelle Lösung*
Destination:	
Arrival:	
Departure:	
No. of people travelling:	
Plans:	

Schritt 3: Ihr Gastgeber möchte Sie gerne bei einem Telefonat besser kennenlernen. Sie machen sich vor dem Gespräch Notizen. Schreiben Sie auf, was Sie ihn gerne fragen möchten:

- Ist die Couch zu Ihren Reisedaten frei? *Individuelle Lösung* ____________________
- Wie weit ist es in das Stadtzentrum? ____________________
- Können Ihre Gastgeber irgendwelche Veranstaltungen oder Sehenswürdigkeiten empfehlen?
  ____
- Wie kommen Sie vom Flughafen zu Ihren Gastgebern? ____________________

Schritt 4: Spielen Sie das Telefonat mit einem Partner/einer Partnerin.

Let's practise → S 2, p. 103

A 26

Welcome to New Zealand

"Kia ora" and "Haere mai"! This means something like "Hello" and "Welcome" in the Maori language. The Maoris are natives of New Zealand. That's where I spent the last 10 months. I worked there as an au pair for a very nice family. My name is Laura Schneider and I am from Germany. After I finished school, I wanted to travel and meet new people so I decided to go to New Zealand. I stayed with a host family in Christchurch and took care of their two children: a 5-year-old boy and a 2-year-old girl. I always made breakfast for them and helped them to get ready for kindergarten. I also helped with some tasks in the house, for example hoovering and cleaning up after meals. But I also had a lot of time to go out and explore the city and meet other young people. And I often went on fun trips with the whole family.
If you want to work as an au pair, it's important that you are patient and friendly. It's also good to have some experience with children. I used to look after my brothers when they were still little, and in the summer I sometimes helped in a summer camp for children.

3 **native** *Ureinwohner/-in* – 11 **to hoover** *Staubsaugen*

a) *Kreuzen Sie an: richtig oder falsch?*

	richtig	falsch
1. Maori sind die Ureinwohner Australiens.	☐	☒
2. Laura verbrachte zehn Monate in Neuseeland.	☒	☐
3. Die Gastfamilie hat ein Kind.	☐	☒
4. Laura musste auch im Haushalt helfen.	☒	☐
5. Die Familie machte oft Ausflüge mit Laura.	☒	☐
6. Um als Au-Pair zu arbeiten, braucht man keine Erfahrung.	☐	☒

b) Complete the sentences.

1. "Kia ora" means _hello_ in the Maori language.
2. After she finished school, Laura wanted to _travel and meet new people_.
3. Laura's host family has a _5-year-old_ boy and a _2-year-old_ girl.
4. It's important to have some _experience_ if you want to work as an au pair.
5. Laura volunteered in a _summer camp_ for children.

c) *Mediation: Sie haben auf einer Website den Bericht von Laura entdeckt und möchten einer Freundin/einem Freund in einer E-Mail davon berichten. Schreiben Sie die E-Mail auf Deutsch. Schreiben Sie über folgende Punkte:* → S 9, p. 110

- *warum hat Laura als Au-Pair gearbeitet?*
- *beschreiben Sie Lauras Gastfamilie*
- *nennen Sie Lauras Tätigkeiten*
- *welche Voraussetzungen braucht man als Au-Pair?*

Individuelle Lösung

4 The right placement for me

j827pv

A

B

C

D

E

F

1 Where do people work?

a) Match ⇄ the words and the pictures. 3 words don't match a picture.
Ordnen Sie die Wörter den Bildern zu. 3 Wörter passen zu keinem Bild.

A in a brewery	– in a factory	C in a garden
F in a kindergarten	– in a restaurant	B in a gym
D in a surgery	E in a kitchen	– in an office

Am Ende der Unit kann ich ...

- ☐ sagen, was ich gut kann.
- ☐ Stellenanzeigen verstehen.
- ☐ sagen, was ich beruflich machen möchte.

At the end of this unit I can ...

- ☐ talk about the things I'm good at.
- ☐ understand job adverts.
- ☐ say what job I want to do.

b) Where do you do these things? Match ⇄ the activities with the right workplace.
Wo macht man diese Dinge? Ordnen Sie die Aktivitäten den richtigen Arbeitsplätzen zu.

kitchen | factory | kindergarten | surgery | garden

1. look after children: kindergarten
2. cook something: kitchen
3. work outside: garden
4. make appointments: surgery
5. work with your hands: factory

c) Look at the workplaces in exercise a). Where would you like to work? Why?
Schauen Sie sich die Arbeitsplätze in Aufgabe a) an. Wo würden Sie gerne arbeiten? Warum?

Individuelle Lösung

You say ...

I would like to work in a kindergarten because I like children.
I would like to work in a kitchen because cooking is fun.
I think working in a surgery is nice because you help people.

2 Listening: Let me tell you about my job! → S 7, p. 108

Working is stressful and boring? Not if you have the right job! Mike, Anna and Tom will tell you something about their work and what they like about it. You will also find out which qualities they need.

A 27 a) Listen to the text. Who does which job?
Hören Sie sich den Text an. Wer macht welchen Job?

1. Mike works as a gardener.
2. Anna works as a nursery school teacher.
3. Tom works as a cook.

b) Find out which qualities Mike, Anna and Tom need for their jobs. Complete the text. → ◯ p. 86
Finden Sie heraus, welche Eigenschaften Mike, Anna und Tom für ihre Jobs brauchen. Vervollständigen Sie den Text.

1. Mike likes being outside. Sometimes he has to work hard. He likes working with his hands and is good at working with machines.
2. Anna loves spending time with children. She is patient and caring. She enjoys playing games with the kids, but she also has to comfort the children when they are sick.
3. Tom loves working with food and being creative. As a cook he needs to be quick and hard-working. He also needs to be able to work in a team.

c) Complete the sentences. One word does not match.
Vervollständigen Sie die Sätze. Ein Wort passt nicht.

polite | organized | helpful | patient | good at languages | caring

1. When you keep calm when you're surrounded by lively children you are patient.
2. When you work in a restaurant and have rude customers you still need to be polite.
3. When you work in an office and always know where you keep your documents you are organized.
4. When you can talk with people from different countries you are good at languages.
5. When you like to explain things to people you are helpful.

e) Tick ✓ the boxes: What are your qualities? What are you good at?
Kreuzen Sie an: Welche Eigenschaften haben Sie? Was können Sie gut?

- ☐ caring
- ☐ patient
- ☐ polite
- ☐ helpful
- ☐ like being outside
- ☐ good with machines
- ☐ work with hands
- ☐ like talking to people
- ☐ work hard
- ☐ pay attention to detail
- ☐ well organized
- ☐ good at languages

f) Now talk to a partner and find out his / her qualities.
Sprechen Sie mit einem Partner/einer Partnerin und finden Sie seine / ihre Eigenschaften heraus.

You say ...
I like talking to people.
How about you?
I can work hard and I pay attention to detail.
I'm well organized. And you?

A 28

3 Reading: A suitable job → S 2, p. 103

INTERNET

HIKING ADVENTURES

OUTDOOR ADVENTURES FOR SPORTY PEOPLE!

You don't want to spend your time sitting in an office the whole day? You like being outside and meeting new people? Then you should become a tour guide at **HIKING ADVENTURES**! We offer hiking tours all over England to tourists from all over the world!

Cool Enterprises

WANTED: COOL CUSTOMER SERVICE AGENTS

You like talking to people, you are polite and organised – then join us in our call centre at **COOL ENTERPRISES**, the famous ice cream company. We are looking for young people who speak at least two languages and are willing to work at weekends.

ProtectWildLife

COME TO THE WILDERNESS!

ProtectWildLife is offering 4-month-internships in Alaska between May and August. You work with our biologists and vets and help them take care of our animals, the beaches and forests. Send us your application and spend your summer with whales, birds and bears!

4 **hiking tour** *Wandertour* – 6 **customer service** *Kundenservice* – 11 **wilderness** *Wildnis* – 13 **vet** *Tierarzt* – 15 **whale** *Wal*

a) Read the text and answer the questions.
Lesen Sie den Text und beantworten Sie die Fragen.

1. In which job(s) do you work outside?

   tour guide, internship in Alaska

2. In which job(s) do you work with people?

   tour guide, customer service agent, internship in Alaska

3. In which job(s) do you need to be fit?

   tour guide, internship in Alaska

4. In which job(s) do you need to be good at languages?

   tour guide, customer service agent

5. In which job(s) do you work in an office?

   customer service agent

b) Which of the three jobs is suitable for Sam, Emma and Nathan?
Welcher der drei Jobs passt zu Sam, Emma und Nathan?

Sam

- helps in his father's office after school
- speaks English and French
- likes working at the weekends

Emma

- her family has a farm
- loves being outdoors
- wants to become a veterinary assistant
- loves hiking and swimming

Nathan

- goes to the gym and plays football
- good with people

Sam: *Wanted: cool customer service agents*

Emma: *Come to the wilderness*

Nathan: *Outdoor adventures for sporty people*

c) Look at the qualities you ticked in exercise e) on page 48. Which of the jobs could be suitable for you? Talk to a partner.
Schauen Sie sich an, welche Eigenschaften Sie in Aufgabe e) auf Seite 48 angekreuzt haben. Welcher der Jobs könnte für Sie passend sein? Sprechen Sie mit einem Partner / einer Partnerin.

Example: I like being outside so I think the job at HIKING ADVENTURES could be suitable.

Your task

Sie sind auf einer Jobbörse und finden den Stand der YOUR-JOB-AGENCY. Diese vermittelt Praktikumsplätze und Ferienjobs im Ausland. Das ist Ihre Gelegenheit, mehr über die Jobmöglichkeiten im Ausland zu erfahren. Die Standmitarbeiter sprechen nur Englisch – Rebecca und Andrew zeigen Ihnen, wie Sie sich auf so ein Gespräch vorbereiten.

Meet the experts

V 8

A 29, 30

1 TUTORIAL Looking at job adverts → S 3, p. 104

a) Before you watch the tutorial: read the advert and answer the questions.
Bevor Sie das Tutorial anschauen: Lesen Sie die Anzeige und beantworten Sie die Fragen.

1. Where is the job? Australia
2. Which job is it? Wombat babysitter
3. Which qualities do you need? Sensitive and caring
4. How can you apply? Send an email to Ruby

Wombat Island Tourism (Australia) is looking for a

WOMBAT BABYSITTER

Wombyhe baby wombat needs some love and cuddles! He's been all alone since his mother was hit by a car and he was brought to our animal shelter.

Do you love animals? Are you a sensitive and caring person? Then contact us! We will pay for your flight to the island and you can also bring a friend.

To apply for the job you can send an email to Ruby from Wombat Island Tourism: ruby@wombat…com.

3 **cuddle** *Kuscheleinheit;* **animal shelter** *Tierheim*

b) Complete the pros and cons of the job.
Vervollständigen Sie die Vor- und Nachteile des Jobs.

1. You can visit another country.
2. It will be boring on the island.
3. The wombat is very cute.
4. The organization will pay for the flight.
5. You will have a nice time on the island.

c) Who said what? Tick ✗✓ the right box.
Wer hat was gesagt? Kreuzen Sie das richtige Kästchen an.

	Andrew	Rebecca
1. "The wombat is so cute."	X	
2. "I won't come with you to the island."		X
3. "I would like to go to Australia."	X	
4. "Wombat Island Tourism will pay for the plane ticket."	X	
5. "There is nobody on the island."		X

2 TUTORIAL Finding the right summer job

V 9

A 31, 32

a) Read the job advert and then watch the video.
Lesen Sie die Stellenanzeige und sehen Sie sich dann das Video an.

Swedish Tourism is looking for

Island Caretakers

Do you like to be outside a lot? Are you friendly and outgoing? Do you like meeting new people and working in a team? Then come to Sweden!

We are looking for helpers to join us on our little island 80 km outside of Stockholm this summer: you will help us to keep the beaches clean and help tourists to find their way around the island.

After a couple of weeks you may get the chance to lead your own team of helpers. In return for your work you will get free bed and board in a cozy cabin by the lake.

Note: online applications accepted only. Please send your application, including CV to Sofia: Swedish_island@...se

4 **outgoing** *kontaktfreudig* – 9 **to find one's way around** *sich zurechtfinden* – 10 **board** *hier: Verpflegung*; **cozy** *gemütlich*

b) What did Andrew and Rebecca say? Complete the sentences. → G 7, p. 96
Was haben Andrew und Rebecca gesagt? Vervollständigen Sie die Sätze.

1. Rebecca: The job in Sweden *will be* (be) outdoors.
2. Andrew: The flight *won't be* (not be) expensive.
3. Andrew: The job *will look* (look) good in my CV.
4. Rebecca: Looks like they *won't pay* (not pay) you any money.
5. Andrew: I *will make* (make) a list of ideas next weekend.
6. Rebecca: You *won't* (will not) have to pay for your room.

You say ...
I think the sun will shine today.
It's raining today so we won't go to the park.

c) Andrew made a list of things he likes and often does or did. Tick ✗ the ones that he should put in his application for the job in Sweden.
Andrew hat eine Liste gemacht mit Dingen, die er mag und oft macht oder gemacht hat. Kreuzen Sie an, welche Dinge er in seiner Bewerbung für den Job in Schweden erwähnen sollte.

- [ ] good at maths
- [x] loves to be outdoors
- [x] cleaned parks for a school project
- [x] loves to meet people
- [x] speaks French
- [ ] worked as a waiter
- [ ] trains a football team
- [x] good at reading maps
- [ ] reads a lot

A 33 3 TUTORIAL Making arrangements on the phone

a) *Kreuzen Sie an: richtig oder falsch?*

	richtig	falsch
1. Andrew spricht am Telefon mit Sofia.	X	
2. Andrew wird im September nach Schweden fliegen.		X
3. Andrew möchte fünf Wochen in Schweden bleiben.		X
4. Sofia wird Andrew mit dem Kleinbus vom Flughafen abholen.	X	
5. Es wird vier Teams mit Helfern geben.	X	
6. Andrew wird im Infocenter arbeiten.		X

● **b)** Correct the wrong statements from task a).
Korrigieren Sie die falschen Aussagen aus Übung a)

Satz Nr. 2: Andrew wird im Juli nach Schweden fliegen.

Satz Nr. 3: Andrew möchte vier Wochen in Schweden bleiben.

Satz Nr. 6: Andrew wird am Strand arbeiten.

● **c)** Listen to the phone call again and complete Andrew's message to a friend in the USA.
Hören Sie sich das Telefongespräch noch einmal an und vervollständigen Sie Andrews Nachricht an einen Freund in den USA.

Hey Dan,

Guess where I will be this *summer*. On an island in *Sweden*!

I have just talked to *Sofia* from *Swedish Tourism*.

The job will start in *July*.

I'll have to take *a sleeping bag* and working clothes with me.

I'll work as a helper on the *beach*.

Okay, I have to go now – I need to book my *flight*!

Andrew

d) Put the words into the correct order. → G 7, p. 96
Bringen Sie die Wörter in die richtige Reihenfolge.

1. Sweden / when / you / will / come to / ?

   When will you come to Sweden?

2. need / what / bring / will / to / I / ?

   What will I need to bring?

3. will / need / I / clothes / working / ?

   Will I need working clothes?

4. July / it / will / be / in / sunny / ?

   Will it be sunny in July?

5. how / helpers / many / will / be / in / team / the / ?

   How many helpers will be in the team?

e) What is Andrew thinking? Match ⇄ the parts of the sentences. → G 8, p. 97
Was denkt Andrew? Verbinden Sie die richtigen Satzhälften.

1. If I get a few days off	it will look good on my CV.
2. If the weather is nice	we will do things together after work.
3. If I become a team leader	I will visit Stockholm.
4. If I meet some nice people	I will apply for a job there after school.
5. If I like Sweden	I will go hiking in my free time.

● **f)** Now you: write two sentences using if-clauses like in task e). → G 8, p. 97
Nun Sie: Schreiben Sie zwei Sätze und benutzen Sie dabei if-clauses wie in Aufgabe e).
Example: If the weather is nice I will meet some friends in the park after school.

Individuelle Lösung

A 34

1 Matt's summer job in a local brewery → S 2, p. 103

It's almost the end of the school year and you're looking for a summer job to earn some money – but you also want to have a good time in your job? Well, Matt will tell you something about his last summer job. Maybe you will find it interesting, too!

"Last year I had a summer job in my local brewery for two months. Of course I was not allowed to brew beer because you need special training for that. But I helped the brewers on the bottling lines – that is the place where the beer is filled into bottles. I had to make sure that there were no broken bottles. Or I had to check that the bottles were closed properly. You have to be focused and pay attention to detail for this task.

I also helped to clean the machines and pack big orders, from restaurants for example. As you can see, you need to be fit to work in a brewery. But there are also some easy tasks: for example I sometimes worked in the little brewery shop. I liked meeting new people and the shop was very popular with local people and tourists – it was perfect!

My colleagues were really nice and helpful! The brewers told me a lot about the brewing process. And who knows: maybe I will look for an apprenticeship to become a brewer after school!"

5 – 6 **bottling line** *Flaschenabfüllung* – 9 **to pack up** *packen* – 12 **popular with** *beliebt bei*

a) Read the text. Find out what Matt tells you about the qualities you need to work in a brewery.

you have to be focused and pay attention to detail; you need to be fit; you need to like meeting new people

b) Pick one of the photos and say what happens on it. Maybe the text will give you some ideas.

Individuelle Lösung

c) Do you think the job is interesting for you? Give three reasons.
Example: I don't think the job is interesting for me because I don't like the smell of beer.

Individuelle Lösung

A 35

2 WANTED: helpers in our youth club

You love children? You are patient and don't mind working in a lively environment? You are sporty or like crafting? Then you are the perfect member for our team!
Our youth club **Cool Kids in Town** is looking for helpers during the school holidays. We offer many activities for children (age 6 – 14) while their parents are at work: playing football or basketball, visiting sights, painting, dancing, team games, making pizza and many more.
If you are at least 18 years old and have some experience working with children we'd love to hear from you!
summerjob@coolkids. . . .uk

2 **crafting** *Basteln* – 5 **painting** *Malen*; **team games** *Mannschaftsspiele*

a) Tick the right boxes: which qualities do you need for the job?

[X] caring	[X] like being outside	[ ] be fit
[X] patient	[X] flexible	[ ] pay attention to detail
[ ] accurate	[X] sensitive	[ ] well organised
[X] helpful	[X] like talking to people	[ ] good at languages

b) Name two other qualities that you need for the job. Pages 47 – 48 at the beginning of this unit will give you some ideas.

for example: friendly, reliable, creative, enjoy playing games, love spending time with children, able to comfort children

c) Is the job interesting for you? Write down reasons.
Example: I think the job is interesting for me because I often spend time with children.

Individuelle Lösung

d) Pick a partner. Tell him / her why the job is interesting for you or not.

Qualities

a) Match ⇄ the qualities with the jobs. There are two qualities for each job.
Ordnen Sie die Eigenschaften den Jobs zu. Zu jedem Job passen zwei Eigenschaften.

tidy | flexible | sensitive | hard-working | patient | friendly | caring | creative | accurate | organized

1. gardener: *hard-working and creative*
2. nursery school teacher: *patient and sensitive*
3. customer service agent: *flexible and friendly*
4. veterinary assistant: *accurate and caring*
5. office assistant: *organized and tidy*

Placements

b) Choose the right beginning of the words.
Wählen Sie den richtigen Wortanfang aus und bilden Sie Wörter.

C / sh / ap / exp / pla / req / appl

1. *exp* erience
2. *sh* ift
3. *ap* ply
4. *pla* cement
5. *C* V
6. *appl* ication
7. *req* uirement

c) Complete the sentences. Use the words in the boxes.
Vervollständigen Sie die Sätze. Verwenden Sie die Wörter in den Kästchen.

comfort / pay attention / required / make appointments / surrounded / surgery

1. Experience with children is *required* if you want to work as an au pair.
2. The little wombat lost his mother so you need to *comfort* him.
3. If you work as a personal assistant you have to *make appointments* for your boss.
4. Workers in a factory have to *pay attention* to details so that the products are good.
5. As a veterinary assistant you are *surrounded* by animals.
6. If you like helping people when they are sick you could work in a *surgery*.

d) Pick the right word and underline it.
Wählen Sie das richtige Wort aus und unterstreichen Sie es.

1. Sometimes the children in our kindergarten hurt themselves, so we need to be caring / accurate.
2. I think this job advert is very interesting. I think I'll answer / apply for the job.
3. The pub is open all day so we work in two parts / shifts.
4. I think the internship will be a very good experience / requirement for me!
5. You should be hard-working and fit if you want to become a caretaker / gardener.

Your turn

Sie sind auf einer Jobbörse und finden den Stand der YOUR-JOB-AGENCY. Diese vermittelt Praktikumsplätze und Ferienjobs im Ausland. Das ist Ihre Gelegenheit, mehr über die Jobmöglichkeiten im Ausland zu erfahren.

A 36

Schritt 1: Wählen Sie eine der drei Stellen aus, die Sie interessiert.

We offer 5 positions as

WAITER / WAITRESS

from June to September in a lively café.

Location: Dublin city centre.
Working hours: day and evening shifts
Requirement: experience is helpful, but not required.

You are friendly and helpful? You like meeting new people? Then we look forward to getting your application!

Apply to:
maryanne@pats… .ie

A

Top hair salon in London is offering placements for

ASSISTANTS

during the summer months.

Your tasks include: greeting customers, serving drinks, making sure towels and supplies are ready for use, keeping the salon clean and tidy.

Are you interested?

Send us an email:
jobs@tophair… .uk

B

Family-run organic farm near Edinburgh is looking for

FARM HELPERS

If you like working outdoors and if you are motivated and fit, you will enjoy working on our farm! We offer food and a nice bed for you in exchange for your help on our farm and in our shop.

Enjoy the summer in Scotland!

organicfamilyfarm@edi… .uk

C

21 **towel** *Handtuch*; **supplies** *hier: Arbeitsutensilien* – 34 **in exchange** *als Gegenleistung*

Schritt 2: Notieren Sie Ihre Stärken und Interessen, die für diese Stelle wichtig sind.

Individuelle Lösung

Schritt 3: Sie treffen auf der Job-Börse einen Mitarbeiter der YOUR-JOB-AGENCY, der nur Englisch spricht, und möchten ihm Fragen stellen. Übersetzen Sie folgende Fragen auf Englisch:

- Wann kann ich anfangen? *When can I start?*
- Wie lange kann ich bleiben? *How long can I stay?*
- Welche Eigenschaften brauche ich? *Which qualities do I need?*
- Wie bewerbe ich mich? *How do / can I apply?*

Schritt 4: Partner A ist ein Jobinteressent, Partner B Mitarbeiter der Agentur. Führen Sie den Dialog.

A 37 **Let's practise!** → S 2, p. 103, S 9, p. 110

The perfect internship!

When Stephen finished school he didn't know what he wanted to do. He didn't want to work in an office and sit inside the whole day. But he also didn't want to work outdoors all the time. "A mix of both would be nice", Stephen thought. One day he read an advert for an internship with a local photographer and he applied because he thought it was interesting. The photographer offered studio photography – for example when people needed new pictures for their passport or wanted to get family portraits – but he also worked outside, for example when he took photos at weddings or festivals. Stephen was lucky: he got the internship and it was a very good experience for him. Stephen was allowed to help the photographer at many different photo shoots inside and outside. He learned a lot about the equipment a photographer uses and the photographer told him interesting things about good lighting and finding the right places to take pictures. Now Stephen is looking for an apprenticeship to become a photographer.

5 **mix** *Mischung* – 11 **passport** *Ausweis, Reisepass* – 17 **equipment** *Ausrüstung* – 19 **lighting** *Beleuchtung*

a) *Kreuzen Sie an: richtig oder falsch?*

	richtig	falsch
1. Stephen möchte am liebsten draußen arbeiten.	☐	☒
2. Der Fotograf arbeitet fast nur im Studio.	☐	☒
3. Das Praktikum war für Stephen eine tolle Erfahrung.	☒	☐
4. Stephen durfte dem Fotografen nur sehr wenig helfen.	☐	☒
5. Stephen sucht nun nach einem Ausbildungsplatz als Fotograf.	☒	☐

b) Match ⇄ the beginnings and the endings of the sentences.

1. Stephen didn't want to … — d. … work outdoors all the time.
2. Stephen read an advert for … — a. … an internship with a photographer.
3. The internship was … — e. … a very good experience.
4. He learned a lot about … — c. … equipment and lighting.
5. Now Stephen … — b. … wants to become a photographer.

c) *Nach seinem Praktikum möchte Stephen seiner Freundin Anna in einer E-Mail von seinen Erfahrungen berichten.*
Schreiben Sie mit den Informationen aus dem Text einen zusammenhängenden Text auf Deutsch in ganzen Sätzen. Schreiben Sie über folgende Punkte:

- *wie ist Stephen zu dem Praktikum beim Fotografen gekommen?*
- *was hat er in seinem Praktikum gemacht?*
- *was hat Stephen im Praktikum gelernt?*
- *welchen Plan hat er für die Zukunft?*

Liebe Anna, wie geht es dir? Mir geht es gut. Ich habe gerade ein Praktikum bei einem Fotografen gemacht. Ich habe die Stellenanzeige für das Praktikum gesehen und mich beworben, weil ich die Stelle interessant fand. Das Praktikum war eine gute Erfahrung für mich: ich durfte dem Fotografen bei Fotoshootings helfen. Außerdem habe ich viel gelernt: über die Ausrüstung eines Fotografen, über gute Beleuchtung und wie man einen guten Ort zum Fotografieren findet. Jetzt möchte ich eine Ausbildungsstelle als Fotograf finden.

Liebe Grüße, Stephen

d) *Am Ende seines Praktikums trifft Stephen seinen ehemaligen Klassenkameraden Josh. Was würde er im folgenden Dialog auf Englisch sagen?*

Josh: Hey Stephen, how are you?

1. Stephen: Mir geht es gut, ich mache gerade ein Praktikum.

   I'm fine. I'm doing an internship at the moment.

   Josh: Oh really? What work do you do?

2. Stephen: Ich arbeite bei einem Fotografen.

   I work with a photographer.

   Josh: Wow, sounds great! What are your tasks?

3. Stephen: Ich helfe dem Fotografen bei Fotoshootings und lerne viel über die Ausrüstung und Beleuchtung.

   I help the photographer at photo shoots and learn a lot about the equipment and lighting.

   Josh: Very interesting. It looks like you are learning a lot! Do you like it?

4. Stephen: Ja, das Praktikum ist eine gute Erfahrung für mich. Ich denke, ich möchte eine Ausbildung zum Fotografen machen.

   Yes, the internship is a good experience for me. I think I would like to do an apprenticeship to become a photographer.

   Josh: I'm happy for you! Look, I have to go now – but let's go for a drink next week!

5. Stephen: Okay, ich werde dich anrufen!

   Okay, I will call you!

   Josh: Perfect, have a nice day!

6. Stephen: Danke, du auch!

   Thanks, you too

e) Stephen's boss tells him some things about the internship. Complete the sentences. Choose the right form of the verbs and use the will-future. → G 7, p. 96

1. "You *will help* (help) me with photo shoots and events like weddings."
2. "Don't worry, you *won't make* (not make) coffee and photocopies!"
3. "I *will tell* (tell) you a lot about my equipment and good lighting."
4. "I think you *will learn* (learn) a lot when you work with me."
5. "Sometimes you *will work* (work) at weekends."
5. "I *won't pay* (not pay) you for the internship."

Culture Tip
When you do an internship, you probably won't earn money – but it will be easier for you to find a job afterwards!

5 Applying for a job

c838kr

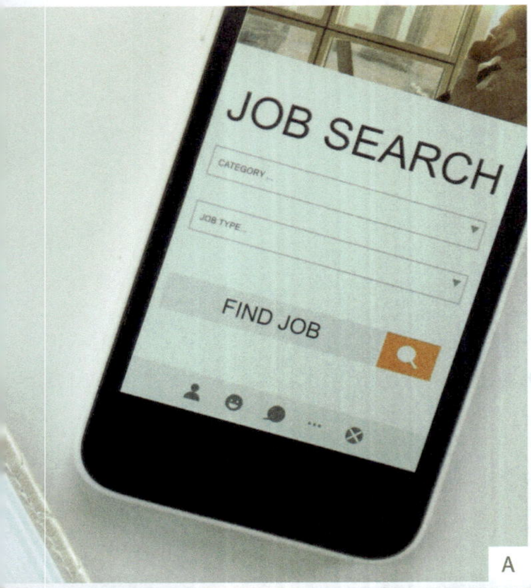

A

B

D

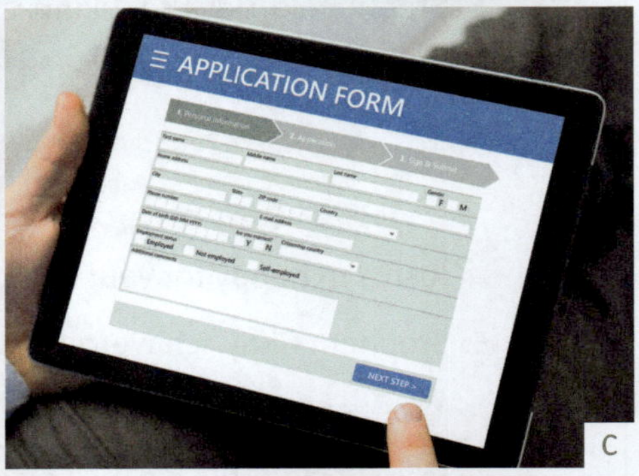

C

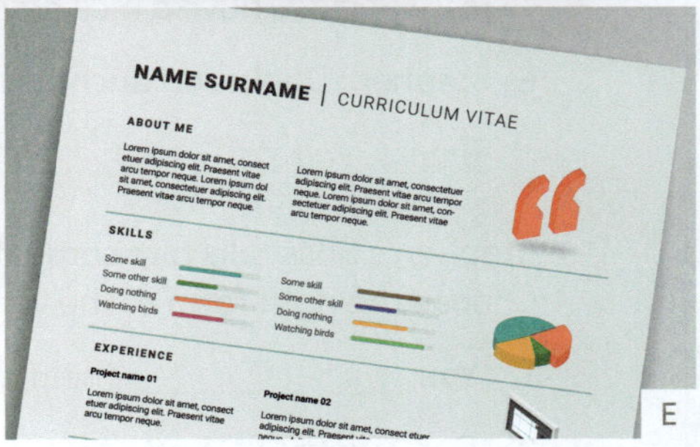

E

1 From advert to interview

a) Match ⇄ the photos and the words.
Ordnen Sie die Fotos den richtigen Begriffen zu.

1. a letter ____
2. a job application *C*
3. an interview *B*
4. a contract ____
5. an employment office *D*
6. a job website *A*
7. a CV *E*
8. a phone interview ____
9. a job advert ____

Am Ende der Unit kann ich ...

- ein Bewerbungsanschreiben verfassen.
- einen Lebenslauf schreiben.
- ein kurzes Vorstellungsgespräch führen.

At the end of this unit I can ...

- write a job application.
- write a CV.
- do a short job interview.

b) Look at the definitions. Write down the correct word from exercise a).
Schauen Sie sich die Definitionen an. Notieren Sie das richtige Wort aus Aufgabe a).

1. A meeting between the candidate and the company *a job interview*
2. Information about schools, work experience, skills *a CV*
3. A phone call in which the candidate answers questions *a phone interview*
4. A place where you get information about jobs *an employment office*
5. A short text about a job *a job advert*
6. A list of questions *an application form*

1 **candidate** *Bewerber/in*

2 Listening: A podcast by a trainee team assistant → S7, p. 108

A 38

Jenny Sievers works for a company that organizes events around the world. The company has put a podcast by Jenny on their website.

Listen to Jenny's podcast and choose one of the exercises a) and b).
Hören Sie Jennys Podcast an und wählen Sie eine der Aufgaben a) und b) aus.

a) Underline the correct information.
Unterstreichen Sie die richtigen Informationen.

1. Jenny macht eine Ausbildung / ein Praktikum / ein Studium bei *GoGlobal Fairs*.
2. Sie hat Adressen bei der Messeagentur / *GoGlobal Fairs* / der Agentur für Arbeit bekommen.
3. Jenny hat mit ihrer Freundin eine Liste mit Stärken / Schwächen / Fähigkeiten geschrieben.
4. Sie hat einen Job bei *GoGlobal Fairs* / im Messezentrum / bei der Agentur für Arbeit gehabt.
5. Sie hat eine englische Bewerbung / einen englischen Lebenslauf / eine englische Bewerbung und einen englischen Lebenslauf geschrieben.
6. Sie hat ein Bewerbungsgespräch vor Ort / ein telefonisches Bewerbungsgespräch / einen Probearbeitstag durchlaufen.

OR

b) Complete the sentences about Jenny. → ◯ p. 86
Vervollständigen Sie die Sätze über Jenny.

1. Jenny is training to be a team *assistant* with a company that organizes events.
2. She got the addresses of companies from her local employment *office*.
3. With the help of a friend, Jenny wrote a list of her *skills*.
4. Her work *experience* at the exhibition hall looked good in her CV.
5. Jenny wrote an *English* application and a CV.
6. She had to do a *phone* interview with *GoGlobal Fairs*.

c) Have you ever done an interview? How was it? Tell a partner about it.
Hatten Sie schon einmal ein Vorstellungsgespräch? Wie war es?
Erzählen Sie einem Partner/einer Partnerin darüber.

d) Complete Jenny's answers to the questions. Use the third form of the verbs. → G9, p. 97
Vervollständigen Sie Jennys Antworten auf die Fragen. Verwenden Sie die 3. Form des Verbs.

work have meet help send

1. Have you ever worked in event organization?

Jenny: No, I've never _had_ a job in event organization.

2. Have you written a job application in English before?

Jenny: No, but I've _sent_ a lot of applications in German.

3. How long have you been a team assistant?

Jenny: I've _worked_ here for six months.

4. What have you learned at *GoGlobal Fairs*?

Jenny: Well, I've already _helped_ to organize two events.

5. Have you spoken a lot of English at *GoGlobal Fairs?*

Jenny: Yes, because I've _met_ a lot of English customers.

You say ...

Jenny has worked a lot this week.
I haven't talked to her since the weekend.
We haven't met for a long time.

3 Reading: Applying for a job → S 2, p. 103

A 39

Jenny tells her friend Simon, about her job and he also applies to *GoGlobal Fairs*.

E-MAIL

Dear Sir or Madam,

I have seen the job advert on your website for a trainee team assistant. I wish to apply for this job.

I am 18 years old and I am doing a business course at a vocational college in Strasbourg in France. I will finish in June this year.

As you can see from my CV I have work experience as a sales assistant in a wine shop. I have worked there at weekends since last summer. I can deal with customers politely and efficiently. The shop is busy and the hours are very long. I have learned to work well under pressure. I am good at English and German.

I can attend a job interview at any time.

I look forward to hearing from you.

Yours sincerely,
Simon Floret

3 **France** *Frankreich* – 7 **pressure** *Druck* – 11 **Yours sincerely** *Mit freundlichen Grüßen*

a) Read Simon's e-mail and tick the right box: true or false?
Kreuzen Sie das richtige Kästchen an: richtig oder falsch?

	true	false
1. Simon bewirbt sich als Verkäufer.	☐	☒
2. Simon besucht ein Berufskolleg.	☒	☐
3. Simon kann höflich und effizient mit Kunden umgehen.	☒	☐
4. Simon ist gut in Englisch und Mathe.	☐	☒
5. Simon ist es gewohnt, lange zu arbeiten.	☒	☐

b) Match the English sentences with the German translations.
Ordnen Sie die englischen Sätze den deutschen Übersetzungen zu.

1. I have seen the job advert on your website.
2. I wish to apply for this job.
3. I am doing a course at a vocational college.
4. I am good at English and maths.
5. I can attend a job interview at any time.
6. I look forward to hearing from you.

a) Ich besuche einen Kurs an einem Berufskolleg.
b) Ich stehe jederzeit für ein Bewerbungsgespräch zur Verfügung.
c) Ich bin gut in Englisch und Mathe.
d) Ich möchte mich um diese Stelle bewerben.
e) Ich freue mich, von Ihnen zu hören.
f) Ich habe die Jobanzeige auf Ihrer Internetseite gesehen.

c) Complete the CV for Mark. Use the words in the boxes.
Vervollständigen Sie den Lebenslauf für Mark. Verwenden Sie die Wörter in den Kästchen.

Saturday | trainer | weeks | team | speak | course

Name:	Mark Loftus
Address:	14, Bridge Street, Epsom
Education:	2015-2018: Business *course*, Epsom College
Work experience:	2017: Work placement for two *weeks* at a transport company
	2016-now: *Saturday* job in a supermarket
Interests:	*trainer* of junior football team at local sports club
	play football for under 21 *team*
Other qualifications:	driving licence, *speak* fluent German

Your task

Bei einer internationalen Firma, die Festivals organisiert und durchführt, wird viel Englisch gesprochen und geschrieben.
Sie möchten sich bei dieser Firma bewerben und sich auf ein Bewerbungsgespräch vorbereiten.
Kein Problem! Rebecca, Andrew, Benjamin und Emily zeigen Ihnen, wie man das auf Englisch macht.

Meet the experts

1 TUTORIAL Dos and don'ts at a job interview → S 3, p. 104

V 10

A 40

a) Put the tips into the order you hear them.
Bringen Sie die Tipps in die Reihenfolge, in der Sie sie hören.

Preparing for an interview

2 Check the company website.
4 Make notes.
3 Check your letter of application.
1 Look at the job advert again carefully.
5 Think about your outfit.

b) Tick the photos that are not suitable for a job interview.
Kreuzen Sie die Fotos an, die für ein Vorstellungsgespräch nicht passen.

A

X

B

X

C

☐

D

X

c) Match the rules and the photos in exercise b). Two rules are not shown.
Ordnen Sie die Regeln den Fotos in Aufgabe b) zu. Zwei Regeln sind nicht auf den Fotos zu sehen.

Rules

B Wear suitable clothes.
___ Turn off your phone.
D Be on time.
C Smile and be polite.
A Finish your coffee before the interview.
___ Make a good first impression.

d) Think of more interview tips. Write a list. → ◯ p. 87
Schreiben Sie weitere Tipps für ein Jobinterview auf. Machen Sie eine Liste.

DOS	DON'TS
Individuelle Lösung	*Example:* Don't chew gum.
	Don't …

Culture Tip
Im Deutschen sagt man: „An der Ampel links **abbiegen.**"
Im Englischen sagt man "**Could you turn left** at the lights, please?" **NIEMALS:** "~~Turn left~~!"

V 11

A 41

2 TUTORIAL Doing a good job interview

a) Tick ✗ the sentences you hear in the tutorial.
Kreuzen Sie die Sätze an, die Sie im Tutorial hören.

- [ ] What are you good at?
- [x] Why do you want to work for us?
- [ ] What do you do in difficult situations?
- [x] Why should we choose you?
- [x] Tell me something about yourself.
- [ ] Why do you want this job?
- [ ] What do you like about your job?
- [x] Do you have any questions?

b) Who said what? Andrew (A) or Rebecca (R).
Wer hat was gesagt? Andrew (A) oder Rebecca (R).

1. "I'm doing a course at a vocational college." R: Rebecca
2. "You earn good money and you have flexible working hours." A: Andrew
3. "I don't mind which company I work for." A: Andrew
4. "I would learn a lot working with you." R: Rebecca
5. "I really enjoyed working in a team." R: Rebecca
6. "Are we finished?" A: Andrew

● c) What do you think? Who will get the job? Why?
Was meinen Sie? Wer wird eingestellt? Warum?

You say ...
I think ... will get the job because ...
I think ... won't get the job because ...

d) Complete the sentences. Use the correct form of the verbs in brackets. → G9, p. 97
Vervollständigen Sie die Sätze. Verwenden Sie die richtige Form des Verbs in Klammern.

1. Rebecca: "I have been (be) to some of your events."
2. Andrew: "I have worked (work) as a bike courier for six months."
4. Rebecca: "I have helped (help) to organize a summer training camp."
5. Rebecca: "I have read (read) your advert."
6. Rebecca: "I think that I have done (do) a good interview."

A 42

1 Make-up artist: Sean's blog → S 2, p. 103

Sean's blog

A make-up artist

Hi, my name is Sean. I come from Leeds in England but I'm living in Düsseldorf now. Last year I started training as a hairdresser in a salon in Düsseldorf. At the beginning I only served coffee and water to the clients. I also did a lot of cleaning and my hands were very dry after the first week. I am learning how to cut and dye hair. I'm not allowed to work with clients yet but I try to watch the other hairdressers at work. I am also learning a lot about make-up. I started training as a make-up artist a week ago. It is so much fun! But it is also hard work! I do an evening course on Mondays and Thursdays from 6 to 9. The course lasts one and a half years. I pay € 650 a month. At the beginning we learn about different make-up and brushes. In the course we also learn to do body painting and photo shoots. We even learn how to photoshop the pictures after the shoots. Next week my class is going to the exhibition hall in Düsseldorf. The theme is hair and make-up and we will see famous models from Paris and London. This job is so interesting! My German has improved a lot since I started my training but I also have to speak English a lot at work.

8 **to dye** *färben* – 9 **I'm not allowed** *ich darf nicht* – 13 **to last** *dauern* – 14 **brush** *Pinsel* – 15 **to photoshop** *Bilder bearbeiten* – 16 **theme** *Thema* – 18 **to improve** *sich verbessern*

a) Look at the pictures and write down the task. Use some of the following words.

to do a photo shoot | to cut hair | to put on make-up | to learn about brushes | to style hair

A *to put on make-up*

B *to style hair*

C *to do a photo shoot*

b) Complete the sentences. → ○ p. 87

1. The training course is on *Mondays* and *Thursdays* from 6 to 9 p.m.
2. The course lasts *one and a half* years.
3. The trainee has to pay *€ 650* a month.
4. A make-up artist learns how to *photoshop* pictures as well.
5. A make-up artist meets famous *models.*

c) Is the job of a make-up artist interesting or not? Give three reasons.

Example: The job is interesting because you learn about make-up.

You learn how to do body painting. You learn how to photoshop photos after a photo shoot.

1 Finding a job

Find nine words or collocations in the word search →↓. → S 4, p. 105
Finden Sie neun Wörter und Verbindungen.

D	I	N	T	E	R	V	I	E	W	Y	M	J	B	Q	Z	Z
Y	P	D	X	Q	F	A	M	O	H	U	S	O	J	T	H	N
Z	P	R	C	O	M	P	A	N	Y	W	E	B	S	I	T	E
R	C	Z	V	W	H	P	Q	F	X	U	B	A	D	S	Y	J
T	P	Y	B	O	Q	L	S	W	A	H	X	D	J	Q	R	F
U	O	X	S	H	Q	Y	W	A	X	F	L	V	Y	L	G	L
X	L	W	O	R	K	E	X	P	E	R	I	E	N	C	E	U
W	I	W	Q	U	O	P	H	B	E	K	M	R	F	Z	X	E
N	T	N	H	K	A	P	P	L	I	C	A	T	I	O	N	N
G	E	Z	R	D	U	I	E	Z	M	G	R	Y	L	D	T	T

Words:

1. a pplication
2. j ob advert
3. c ompany website
4. C V
5. a pply
6. i nterview
7. p olite
8. w ork e xperience
9. f luent

2 Talking about jobs

a) Match ⇄ the words with their definitions.
Ordnen Sie die Wörter den Definitionen zu.

1. to earn
2. to train
3. to apply
4. to deal with
5. to prepare

a) to learn how to do a job
b) to talk to
c) to make money from a job
d) to get ready for something
e) to write an e-mail / a letter asking for a job

b) Complete the words for the jobs.
Vervollständigen Sie die Wörter.

1. t e a m a ssist a nt
2. b i k e cour i e r
3. s ale s a s s istant
4. t rai n e e
5. h a i rdr e ss e r
6. ma k e-u p a r tis t

c) Match ⇄ the two words that go together.
Bringen Sie die beiden richtigen Wörter zusammen.

1. exhibition
2. work
3. trade
4. event
5. driving

a) organization
b) fair
c) hall
d) licence
e) placement

Your turn

A 43 Bei einer internationalen Firma, die Festivals organisiert und durchführt, wird viel Englisch gesprochen. Sie möchten sich bei dieser Firma bewerben und sich auf ein Bewerbungsgespräch vorbereiten.

INTERNET

GoGlobal Fairs

You are good at organizing? You are creative and good at languages? You like working with other people? Then WE have the right job for you!

As our team assistant you can help to plan and prepare events. You often have to go to trade fairs and events and work long hours. You also have to work in a team and cooperate with the people you work with.

As we are an international company, you need to speak English with most of the people at work. We will test your English language skills in a phone interview.

Interested? Send your English application and CV to info@goglobalfairs

Schritt 1: Lesen Sie sich die Jobanzeige durch.

Schritt 2: Schauen Sie den Notizzettel von Rebecca an, den sie vor dem Vorstellungsgespräch geschrieben hat.

Rebecca

- 18 years old
- course at a college
- good at working in a team, helped to organize a summer training camp last year
- interests: do a lot in a local youth club
- work experience: part-time work as a sales assistant
- don't smoke

Schritt 3: Machen Sie sich einen eigenen Spickzettel.

You

- age: ______________________________
- school: ______________________________
- good at: ______________________________
- interests: ______________________________
- work experience: ______________________________

Schritt 4: Drehen Sie ein kurzes Video über sich selbst. Verwenden Sie dafür Ihren Spickzettel und die Redemittel im „You say-Kästchen“.

● **Schritt 5:** Schreiben Sie Ihren eigenen Lebenslauf. Sie können Marks Lebenslauf auf Seite 63 als Beispiel nehmen.

You say …

Hello my name is …
I am doing (name of course at college)
I am really good at …
I am very interested in …
I have worked in …

Individuelle Lösung

● **Schritt 6:** Finden Sie einen Partner / eine Partnerin und machen Sie ein kurzes Rollenspiel zum Thema Vorstellungsgespräch am Telefon. Einigen Sie sich auf drei Interview-Fragen und bereiten Sie die Antworten mit Ihrem Partner / Ihrer Partnerin vor. Verwenden Sie dafür Ihren Lebenslauf.

Interview-Fragen

Can you please tell me about yourself?
Why do you want to work for us?
Why should we choose you for the job?
What work experience do you have?
Do you have any questions?

You say …

Student A:
- (name) from *GoGlobal Fairs* speaking.
- How are you?
- Can I ask you some questions?
- It was nice talking to you.
- We will contact you …

You say …

Student B:
- This is (name).
- I'm fine, thank you.
- Could you repeat that, please?
- It was nice talking to you, too.
- Thank you for calling.

A 44

Let's practise → S 2, p. 103, S 7, p. 108

Name:	Matthew Barclay
Address:	15 Oxford Square, London E1 8LL Great Britain
Tel. no.:	+ 44 20 555 692
Mobile no.:	+ 44 151 634 88 94
Email:	matthew@barclay.uk
Nationality:	British
Education:	secondary school in London (7 years)
Work experience:	
2015	3 months (July-September) at a fast-food restaurant
2016	work placement for six months as a team assistant at *GoGlobal Fairs* in Essen, Germany
Interests:	travelling, languages, helping to organize sports camps
Additional qualifications:	full driving licence fluent in German

7 **secondary school** *weiterführende Schule* – 9 **fast-food restaurant** *Schnellimbiss*

Culture Tip
Im englischen Lebenslauf muss man seinen Familienstand und sein Alter nicht angeben.

a) Read the CV. Tick ✗ the correct box: true or false?
Lesen Sie den Lebenslauf. Kreuzen Sie an: richtig oder falsch?

	richtig	falsch
1. Matthew wohnt in Birmingham.	☐	X
2. Er hat die Sekundarstufe I abgeschlossen.	X	☐
3. Er hat 2015 in Teilzeit für eine Fastfood-Kette gearbeitet.	X	☐
4. Er hat in Deutschland ein sechsmonatiges Praktikum gemacht.	X	☐
5. Er macht gerne Sport und ist gut in Mathematik.	☐	X
6. Er hilft bei der Organisation von Messen.	☐	X
7. Er hat einen Führerschein.	X	☐
8. Er spricht fließend Italienisch und Spanisch.	☐	X

Listen to Jenny's interview with *GoGlobal Fairs* and choose one of the exercises.
Hören Sie Jennys Interview mit GoGlobal Fairs *und wählen Sie eine der Aufgaben aus.*

A 45 **b)** Tick ✗✓ the questions Jenny is asked.
Hören Sie sich Jennys Interview mit GoGlobal Fairs an. Kreuzen Sie die Fragen an, die Jenny gestellt werden.

- [X] Can you tell me about your work experience?
- [X] Why do you want to work for *GoGlobal Fairs*?
- [X] Why should we give you the job?
- [ ] Who are you?
- [ ] What will you do if we don't give you the job?
- [ ] What are your skills?
- [X] Do you have any questions?
- [X] Could you tell me what you are doing at the moment?

OR

● **c)** Answer the questions in complete sentences.
Beantworten Sie die Fragen in ganzen Sätzen. → ○ p. 87

1. What is Jenny doing at the moment? *She is doing a one-year business course at a vocational college.*
2. Why does she want to work for *GoGlobal Fairs*? *They are an interesting company. They organize events around the world and they offer a good training programme.*
3. List three of Jenny's skills. *She is well organized, good at languages and doesn't mind working long hours.*
4. What question does Jenny ask? *When does the job start?*
5. When will Mr Malone call Jenny? *He will call her in two weeks.*

d) You have read the job advert of *GoGlobal Fairs* on page 68. You want to apply for this job.
Write an e-mail to *GoGlobal Fairs* in about 60 words in complete English sentences.

Tell them
- why you are writing
- who you are and which school you go to
- what work experience and skills you have
- when you can attend an interview

Individuelle Lösung

6 On the job

t7f26i

A

B

C

D

E

F

1 What's the problem?

a) Look at the photos. Match ⇄ the problems with the photos. Three problems do not match.
Schauen Sie sich die Bilder an. Ordnen Sie die Probleme den Bildern zu. Drei Probleme passen nicht.

1. difficult ____	2. ill ____	3. tired B
4. broken F	5. stressed E	6. late C
7. not dressed properly A	8. lonely ____	9. badly organized D

Am Ende der Unit kann ich …

- über meine beruflichen Pläne sprechen.
- auf Beschwerden reagieren.
- mit Problemsituationen umgehen.

At the end of this unit I can …

- talk about what job I want to do.
- react to complaints.
- deal with difficult situations.

b) Complete the sentences with some of the words in a).
Vervollständigen Sie die Sätze mit einigen Wörtern aus a).

1. Tina was late for work on Monday and Wednesday this week.
2. Can you help me? The photocopier is broken.
3. Are you still looking for that paper? You're so badly organized, Peter!
4. There is so much work at the moment. I feel really stressed.
5. You can't go to the office like that. I think you're not dressed properly.
6. I started work at 7 and now I'm really tired.

c) What do you say in a difficult situation? Match ⇄ the questions with the right answers.
Was sagen Sie in einer schwierigen Situation? Verbinden Sie die Fragen mit den richtigen Antworten.

1. Why are you late for work? — d)
2. Do I have to do this task? I'm really busy. — c)
3. I think this tool is broken. Do you have another one? — f)
4. Laura, can you please wear some nicer jeans tomorrow? — e)
5. Can I please go for lunch with you? I'm new here and I feel a bit lonely. — b)
6. Have you seen my notebook? I'm badly organized. — a)

a) Oh dear. Maybe you left it in the meeting room earlier.
b) Sure! Meet us at the front desk at 12:30.
c) I'm sorry but it's really important. You can ask Mike to help you.
d) It won't happen again. I'll get an earlier train tomorrow.
e) Yes, of course. I was in a hurry this morning. I'm sorry I didn't dress right.
f) Oh, you're right. I'll get you a different one.

d) Complete the dialogue in the phone shop. Use some of the sentences in the boxes.
Vervollständigen Sie den Dialog im Telefonladen. Verwenden Sie einige Sätze im You-say-Kästchen.

Customer	Sales assistant
I want to make a complaint. I have a problem with this smartphone that I bought here yesterday.	1. I'm sorry to hear that. What's the problem?
It doesn't work.	2. Let me see. Oh dear. You're right. But don't worry, we'll give you a new phone.
I'd like to have a black phone this time.	3. No problem! We will give you a black phone. Have you got the receipt *(Kassenbon)*?
Yes, here you are.	Here's the new phone and it works. 4. It won't happen again.

You say ...
It won't happen again.
Oh dear! You're right.
We will give you a black phone.
No problem!
I'm sorry to hear that.

You say ...
Wenn man einen Lösungsvorschlag macht, verwendet man **will**.
Z. B. We will give you the money back.

A 46

2 Listening: At a hotel

Lara works as a receptionist in a hotel in Munich. She often speaks English with guests because they come from all over the world. She sometimes has to deal with problems in English.

a) Listen to the text. Underline the correct answer.
Hören Sie sich den Text an. Unterstreichen Sie die richtige Antwort.

1. The family comes from England / Sweden / Italy.
2. Their plane was two hours late / on time / five hours late.
3. The taxi was stuck in traffic for fourteen minutes / forty minutes / four hours.
4. The Johanssons have booked a single room / a family room / a double room.
5. The family gets a room with four beds / three beds / one bed.
6. Lara calls the porter / the other receptionist / a waiter to carry the bags.

Sweden *Schweden* – **Italy** *Italien* – **porter** *Gepäckträger*

b) Complete the sentences.
Vervollständigen Sie die Sätze.

1. The family is staying for three nights.
2. The room is not ready.
3. The family gets a new room: room 429.
4. Their room has a nice view of the park.
5. The room is on the fourth floor.

c) Sie arbeiten an der Rezeption eines Hotels. Was sagen Sie auf Englisch, wenn ein Gast sich beschwert? → S 9, p. 110

Guest: Hello, my name is Blake.

You: Guten Morgen, Herr Blake. Kann ich Ihnen helfen?

Good morning, Mr Blake. Can I help you?

Guest: Yes, I've booked a double room for four nights.

You: Ich schaue gleich, Herr Blake. Ich habe nur ein Doppelzimmer vom 1. bis zum 4. April.

Let me have a look, Mr Blake. I only have a double room from April 1 to April 4.

Guest: That can't be right. That's only three nights.

You: Es tut mir leid, Herr Blake. Haben Sie unsere Bestätigung?

I'm sorry, Mr Blake. Do you have our confirmation?

Guest: Yes, here it is. The confirmation says from April 1 to April 5.

You: Sie haben recht. Ich werde schauen, was ich machen kann.

You are right. I'll see what I can do.

Guest: The hotel made the mistake.

You: Es tut mir wirklich leid. Wir haben ein Zimmer mit einem Doppelbett und ein kleines Zustellbett.

I'm really sorry. We have a room with a double bed and an extra small bed.

Guest: That's ok.

You: Vielen Dank, Herr Blake. Der Gepäckträger wird Ihre Taschen aufs Zimmer bringen.

Thank you, Mr Blake. The porter will bring your bags to the room.

A 47 3 Reading: Dos and Don'ts at work

a) Kristin aus Köln hatte heute ihren ersten Tag als Kellnerin in einem Restaurant in Brighton. Von ihrem Chef hat sie die folgende Checkliste bekommen. Abends möchte sie eine E-Mail an ihre Freundin Sarah in Deutschland schreiben und ihr davon berichten.
Schreiben Sie die E-Mail und erzählen Sie von den folgenden Punkten:

- wie soll sich Kristin bei der Arbeit verhalten bzw. nicht verhalten?
- welche Regeln gibt es für Kristins Kleidung?
- welche Aufgaben hat Kristin?
- wie soll Kristin mit Beschwerden umgehen? → S 9, p. 110

Dos

- Be friendly and helpful.
- Smile at guests even if your feet hurt.

- Wear your uniform.
- Your uniform should be clean and properly ironed.
- Keep your hair tidy.
- Wash your hands often.

- Take orders quickly.
- Bring drinks and food to the guests.
- Ask guests if they want to order dessert.
- Bring the bill when guests ask you – and not before.
- Clean tables when guests have left – and not before.

- Deal with complaints in a friendly way. Always say "sorry".

Don'ts

- Don't get nervous when there are a lot of guests in the restaurant.

- Don't wear jewellery.
- Don't have visible tattoos.
- Don't have long nails.

- Don't be unfriendly to guests when there is a lot to do.

- Don't panic if a guest complains.

A waiter or a waitress is the "face" of a restaurant.

3 **to hurt** *wehtun* – 5 **ironed** *gebügelt* – 10 **dessert** *Nachtisch* – 11 **bill** *Rechnung* – 18 **jewellery** *Schmuck* – 19 **visible** *sichtbar* – 20 **nail** *Fingernagel* – 23 **to panic** *in Panik geraten*

- *freundlich und hilfsbereit sein; lächeln; Gäste mit einem Lächeln begrüßen; nicht nervös werden, wenn viele Gäste im Restaurant sind*
- *saubere und gebügelte Berufskleidung tragen*
- *Bestellungen schnell aufnehmen, Getränke und Essen bringen; einen Nachtisch anbieten, Rechnung erst auf Anfrage bringen, Tisch abräumen erst wenn Gäste weg sind*
- *freundlich und ruhig bleiben; sich entschuldigen; nicht in Panik verfallen*

Your task

YOUR-JOB-AGENCY, die Sie in Unit 4 kennengelernt haben, hat Ihnen einen Job im Ausland vermittelt. Die Agentur hat ein Online-Forum, in dem Sie sich mit anderen Jugendlichen, die im Ausland arbeiten, austauschen können.
Einige dieser Jugendlichen erzählen von Konflikten und Problemen im Berufsalltag und Sie möchten ihnen helfen. Kein Problem! Rebecca, Andrew, Benjamin und Emily zeigen Ihnen, wie man sich in Konfliktsituationen verhält.

Meet the experts

A 48 **1** TUTORIAL **Talking about plans** → S 3, p. 104

a) Tick ✗ the correct answer. What is Emily doing?
Kreuzen Sie die richtige Antwort an. Was macht Emily gerade?

Emily is …

☐ 1. cooking dinner ☒ 2. interviewing Benjamin ☐ 3. phoning Benjamin

b) *Unterstreichen Sie die richtige Lösung.*

1. Benjamin wird nach Neuseeland / Australien / Italien gehen.
2. Benjamin wird dort in einem Hotel / Restaurant / Shop arbeiten.
3. Rebecca wird bei einer/m Bäckerei / Cateringunternehmen / Autofirma arbeiten.
4. Rebecca wird in eine eigene Wohnung / in eine WG / in ein Wohnheim ziehen.
5. Andrew wird eine Ausbildung machen / weiter zur Schule gehen / das Schuljahr wiederholen.

c) Fill in the gaps. Use **am going to** / **is going to** / **are going to.** → G 10, p. 98
Ergänzen Sie die Lücken. Verwenden Sie **going to.**

1. Benjamin *is going to visit* (visit) his aunt and uncle.
2. Rebecca is excited about meeting her new flatmates. She *is going to move* (move) to London.
3. "I *am going to stay* (stay) at school and do a business course," said Andrew.
4. Andrew's friends *are going to look* (look) for jobs.
5. Andrew *is going to travel* (travel) before the next school year starts.

excited *aufgeregt* – **flatmate** *Mitbewohner/-in* – **to move** *umziehen*

d) Write negative sentences. Use **am not going to / isn't going to / aren't going to.** → G 10, p. 98
Schreiben Sie negative Sätze. Verwenden Sie **am not going to / isn't going to / aren't going to.**

1. Benjamin wants to learn to surf in the afternoons. He *isn't going to work* (not / work) in the afternoons.
2. His aunt and uncle have offered him a job. They *aren't going to pay* (not / pay) him much.
3. Rebecca has found an apprenticeship in London. She *isn't going to live* (not / live) at home anymore.
4. Andrew's friends want to make money. They *aren't going to go* (not / go) to college next year.
5. Andrew says, "I'm going to travel in the summer." "I*'m not going to have* (not / have) time to work."

V 12
A 49

2 TUTORIAL Dealing with problems with your boss

a) Who said what? Rebecca or Benjamin? One sentence doesn't match.
Ordnen Sie die Sätze Rebecca oder Benjamin zu. Ein Satz passt nicht.

1. "It won't happen again." Benjamin
2. "Why did you come in late?" Rebecca
3. "What's the problem?" ______
4. "That was the problem. The customer was angry." Rebecca
5. "I'm really sorry." Benjamin

b) Tick the right box: true or false?
Kreuzen Sie die richtige Antwort an: richtig oder falsch?

	true	false
1. Benjamin's boss was late for work.	☐	X
2. This is the first time Benjamin has been late.	☐	X
3. Benjamin's bus was late.	☐	X
4. The rest of the team waited for Benjamin.	X	☐
5. The team was thirty minutes late.	☐	X

V 13
A 50

3 TUTORIAL Dealing with a difficult situation

A

B

a) Complete the sentences about the photos.
Vervollständigen Sie die Sätze zu den Fotos.

friendly | helpful | stressed | polite | angry | unhappy

A: Andrew is angry and unhappy and stressed.

B: Emily is polite and helpful and friendly.

b) Complete the sentences. *Ergänzen Sie die Sätze.*

1. Emily works in a hotel.
2. Andrew has booked a room for two nights.
3. The hotel confirmation says that Andrew has booked a king-size bed.
4. The hotel has made a mistake.
5. Breakfast usually costs 15 Euros.
6. Andrew will get a room with a view of the river.

A 51

1 Dealing with people: Ticket office clerk → S 2, p. 103

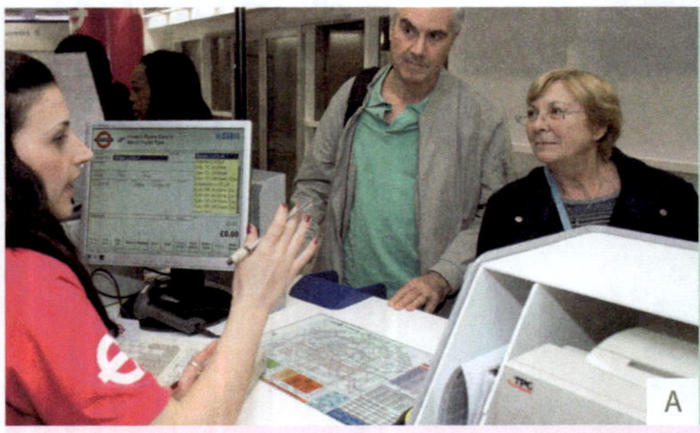
A

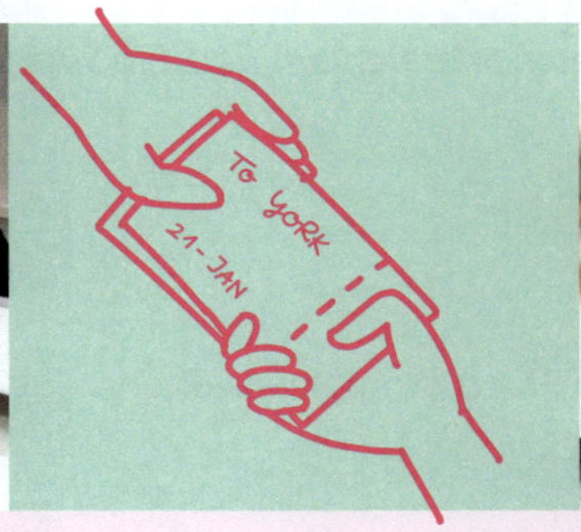

B

Hi I'm Sarah. If you come into my local train station that's where you'll find me – at the ticket desk. My main tasks are to sell tickets and to help people to plan their train journeys.
You meet a lot of nice and interesting people in my job. That's fun because every day is different. There are other aspects of my job that I really like. We wear a really smart uniform. I think that it is important to look good when you meet people. I like being part of a team and I'm well-organized and like to keep my desk tidy.
A big part of the job is when trains are late and I have to deal with customers. When they come to me to complain they are usually angry. I found this situation very difficult at the beginning. I have done some courses and I can now stay quiet and friendly. I always say that I'm sorry and try to find another train connection. Sometimes I change the customer's booking for free when they miss their connection. Most people are happy when you help them.
Oh, and the best thing about my job: I can travel on the train for free any time I want! My boyfriend Matt is training to be a train driver and we want to visit 12 new cities in 12 months. We'll see if we can do it.

1 **ticket desk** *Fahrkartenschalter* – 4 **smart** *schick* – 10 **connection** *Verbindung;* **booking** *Buchung*

a) Read about Sarah's job. What parts of the job are interesting? What parts are difficult?

Interesting parts	Difficult parts
she meets nice and interesting people	*she deals with angry customers*
every day is different	*she must stay quiet and friendly*
she has done courses	*she has to say she is sorry*

b) Sarah sometimes deals with angry customers. What does she say? Choose the correct answer.

Customer

1. Hello, I want to make a complaint.
2. My train from the airport was thirty minutes late.
3. Maybe, but now my connection to London has gone.
4. I have an important meeting in London this afternoon and I can't be late.
5. When will I be in London?
6. Ok, thank you. You have been very helpful.

Sarah

a) That's right, sir. There was a problem with the engine.
b) No, of course not. Here's the next fast connection to London.
c) You're welcome sir. Have a good trip.
d) Oh dear, I'm sorry, sir. I will look for a new connection.
e) Hello, sir. Of course. How can I help you?
f) You'll be there in forty-five minutes.

engine *Triebwerk* – **connection** *Verbindung* – **You're welcome!** *Gern geschehen!*

A 52

2 Dealing with people: Call centre operator

You'll need to ...

- ☐ be friendly.
- ☐ speak clearly.
- ☐ be able to follow instructions.
- ☐ work well under pressure.
- ☐ speak another language (French, Turkish or Russian).

If you can Tick ✓ all of these boxes, then you will be a good call centre operator.

You'll ...

- ☐ answer phone calls and emails from customers
- ☐ deal with complaints
- ☐ offer help and information
- ☐ spend your time at a computer

If you are interested in these tasks, then you will be a good call centre operator.

Apply to callcentre@talk.uk.

You'll also ...

- ☐ do training courses
- ☐ do communication courses
- ☐ learn about quality control

If you take the chance to train properly, then you'll be a good call centre operator and we want to hear from you!

4 **to follow instructions** *Anweisungen befolgen* – 5 **pressure** *Druck* – 6 **French** *Französisch* – 7 **Russian** *Russisch* – 21 **quality control** *Qualitätssicherung*

a) Look at the job advert for a call centre operator. What qualities do you need to have?

You need to be friendly, to speak clearly, to be able to follow instructions, to work well under pressure, to speak another language

b) What parts of the job are interesting? What parts are difficult?

Interesting parts	Difficult parts
offer help	*deal with complaints*
speak another language	*work well under pressure*
do communication courses	

c) Do you think that the job is interesting for you or not?

Individuelle Lösung

1 Talking about people and things

Translate the German words into English and solve the crossword puzzle. → S 4, p. 105
Übersetzen Sie die deutschen Wörter ins Englische und lösen Sie das Kreuzworträtsel.

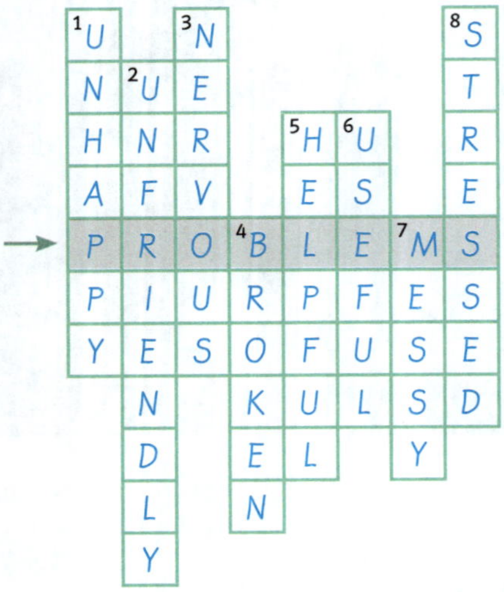

1. unglücklich
2. unfreundlich
3. nervös, aufgeregt
4. kaputt
5. hilfsbereit
6. nützlich
7. unordentlich
8. gestresst

A receptionist in a hotel often has to deal with p r o b l e m s.

2 At a hotel

Complete the sentences. Use the words in the boxes.
Vervollständigen Sie die Sätze. Verwenden Sie die Wörter in den Kästchen.

spend | make | work | deal | book | do | stuck

1. I want to book a double room in your hotel.
2. We want to spend some time in England next summer.
3. Mr Johannsen: "Sorry we're late. We were stuck in traffic."
4. "We're unhappy with the room. We have to make a complaint about it."
5. Receptionist: "Don't worry, I can deal with the problem."
6. Guest: "The phone in my room doesn't work. Can you please do something?"
7. Jill: "I want to do a business course when I finish my summer job in the hotel."

3 People at work

Read the definitions and find the right words.
Lesen Sie die Definitionen und finden Sie die richtigen Wörter.

1. a person you work with is a c o l l e a g u e
2. a person who repairs machines is a t e c h n i c i a n
3. a person who sells train tickets is a t i c k e t o f f i c e c l e r k
4. a person who deals with complaints on the phone is a c a l l c e n t r e o p e r a t o r
5. a person who works in a hotel is a r e c e p t i o n i s t
6. a person who drives a train is a t r a i n d r i v e r

Your turn

YOUR-JOB-AGENCY, die Sie in Unit 4 kennengelernt haben, hat Ihnen einen Job im Ausland vermittelt. Die Agentur hat ein Online-Forum, in dem Sie sich mit anderen Jugendlichen, die im Ausland arbeiten, austauschen können. Einige der Jugendliche erzählen von Konflikten und Problemen im Berufsalltag und Sie möchten ihnen helfen.

Schritt 1: Lesen Sie sich die Probleme im Nutzerforum aufmerksam durch. Wählen Sie einen Beitrag aus, den Sie gerne beantworten würden.

BLOG

Daniel

I am doing a really great apprenticeship in a car company. I work hard but my boss isn't happy with me. Every morning he complains about my workbench. He says it's very messy. I don't think that I'm badly organized. I can find everything. The problem is I don't have time to clean my workbench in the evening. I have to leave work on time to get my bus. What should I do?

Carolyn

Help! What can I do? My mum wants me to give up my Saturday job. She thinks that I need to work harder for school. But I really enjoy the job in the paper shop. I meet a lot of people and the money is very useful. Mum thinks that school is more important.

Adam

I have a job in a hair salon. My problem is that my boss doesn't like my tattoos. When I wear a T-shirt you can see them. But I can't wear a sweatshirt all of the time, it's too hot in the salon. My boss can't fire me because I have tattoos. Or can he? All of the customers like me and they like my tattoos too!

2 **workbench** *Werkbank* – 7 **to enjoy** *Spaß haben*; **paper shop** *Zeitungsladen* – 12 **to fire** *feuern*

Schritt 2: Notieren Sie sich zunächst ein paar Stichpunkte.

Daniel

- boss unhappy
- messy …
- doesn't have time to …
- has to leave …
- has to catch …

Schritt 3: Überlegen Sie sich – mit Ihrem Partner / Ihrer Partnerin – eine Lösung. Verwenden Sie dabei die Sätze im Kästchen. → ◯ p. 88

You say …

I think you should …
Why don't you …?
You could …
The best thing to do is to …

Schritt 4: Schreiben Sie eine Antwort auf das Problem.

● **Schritt 5:** Suchen Sie zwei Partner / -innen, die dasselbe Problem bearbeitet haben. Lesen Sie sich Ihre Lösungen vor. Entscheiden Sie dann, wer die besten Lösungsmöglichkeiten anbietet.

Let's practise → S 2, p. 103, S 7, p. 108, S 9, p. 110

A 53 Sven is doing a placement in a company in England. He writes an e-mail to his teacher, Ms Semmler at his college in Karlsruhe.

E-MAIL

Dear Ms Semmler,

I've done two weeks of my placement here in Brighton and I'm learning a lot.
You know how we talked about England in class at college. Well, things are really different when you live in England! For example, my colleague Matt is nice but he makes jokes that I don't understand. English people and German people don't always find the same things funny.
Matt talks about the weather too all of the time. I think that is normal for English people.
My boss said that I am very direct with customers. I think you need to say what you mean.
My boss thinks it is more polite to say "I'm sorry" or "You're right" even when customers are wrong! My team never gets to work on time. I'm always at my desk ten minutes early and they normally come in five or ten minutes late.
The team is very friendly and I don't feel lonely at all. We sometimes go for a drink after work.
At the beginning I waited for someone to take my order but Matt said that doesn't work. You must order your drink at the bar and pay immediately!
Another thing is that British people love to go shopping. The shops are open every day – even on a Sunday. I prefer to do sports on Sundays but all of the people I know are in the shops.

Best wishes
Sven

7 **direct** *unverblümt* – 16 **Best wishes** *Viele Grüße*

a) *Entscheiden Sie, ob die Aussagen / statements richtig /* true *oder falsch /* false *sind. Kreuzen Sie jeweils an. Verbessern Sie anschließend die falschen Aussagen / statements.*

Aussagen	**richtig**	**falsch**
1. Sven hat vor zwei Wochen ein Praktikum gemacht.	☐	☒
2. Sven versteht die englischen Witze von Matt nicht.	☒	☐
3. Matt spricht die ganze Zeit über die Arbeit.	☐	☒
4. Svens Chef meint, man muss sich nur entschuldigen, wenn man etwas falsch gemacht hat.	☐	☒
Statements	**true**	**false**
5. Sven sometimes gets to work five or ten minutes late.	☐	☒
6. Sven feels good because his team is very friendly.	☒	☐
7. In England you always order your drink at the bar.	☒	☐
8. You can pay for the drink later, before you leave the pub.	☐	☒

Verbesserung: *1. Sven macht seit zwei Wochen ein Praktikum in Brighton.*

3. Matt spricht die ganze Zeit über das Wetter.

4. Sein Chef meint, dass es höflicher ist, sich zu entschuldigen, selbst wenn man nichts falsch gemacht hat.

Correction: *5. Sven is always at his desk ten minutes early.*

8. You should always pay after you have ordered your drink.

b) Complete the sentences. Use only information from the text.

1. Sven is doing his _placement_ in Brighton, England.
2. When you live in England you see that many things are _different_ from Germany.
3. English and German people don't always find the same jokes _funny_.
4. It's quite normal for English people to talk about the _weather_.
5. English shops are _open_ every day, even on Sundays.

c) Could you imagine doing a placement in England? Say why or why not.
Write 40 to 50 words in complete English sentences.

A 54 **d)** Sven is talking to his boss, Mr Blair. Tick the right sentences.

Sven is ...

☐ lonely	☒ always on time	☐ funny	☒ unfriendly
☐ friendly	☒ well organized	☒ direct	☐ messy

● **e)** *Sie hören das Gespräch ein zweites Mal. Ergänzen Sie folgende Aussagen mit den richtigen Fakten.* → ○ p. 88

1. Mr Blair freut sich, weil Sven _pünktlich_ zur _Arbeit kommt_.
2. Sven kommt gerne rechtzeitig, um nicht den ganzen Tag _gestresst zu sein._.
3. Das Praktikum gefällt Sven _gut_.
4. Sven findet, dass in England _manches anders ist_, als er es erwartet hat.
5. Sven erklärt, dass er _viel lernt_.
6. Mr Blair findet, dass Sven gut organisiert ist und gut _im Team_ arbeitet.
7. Sven wird in Zukunft versuchen, zu den Kunden _höflicher zu sein._.
8. Mr Blair ist der Meinung, dass Sven gut _Probleme lösen kann_.

f) **Mediation:** Sven fährt bald wieder nach Hause. Er unterhält sich abends bei einem Drink mit Matt. Was würde er im folgenden Dialog auf Englisch sagen?

Matt: Hey, Sven. I can't believe that you're going to finish tomorrow.
Sven: Ich weiß. Ich habe eine tolle Zeit in Brighton gehabt und viel gelernt.

1. _I know. I've had a great time in Brighton and I've learned a lot._

Matt: What are you going to do next week?
Sven: Ich werde zunächst eine Woche Urlaub machen.

2. _I'm going to go on a holiday for a week._

Matt: Oh great. What are you going to do?
Sven: Ich werde meine Freundin morgen am Flughafen treffen. Wir wollen nach Wales fahren.

3. _I'm going to meet my girlfriend at the airport tomorrow. We want to travel to Wales._

Matt: What are you going to do in Germany? Are you going to look for a job?
Sven: Nein, ich habe mich schon beworben. Ich werde in zwei Wochen bei einem Transportunternehmen anfangen.

4. _No, I've already applied for a job. I'm going to start working for a transport company in two weeks._

Matt: Well done! That sounds great. What kind of job is it?
Sven: Ich werde in einem Büro arbeiten. In den ersten vier Woche werde ich einen Kurs haben.

5. _I'm going to work in an office. I'm going to do a training course in the first four weeks._

Matt: Well cheers!!

Unit 1

2 Listening Seite 7

A 1

b) Underline the correct part of the sentence.
Unterstreichen Sie die richtigen Aussagen.

1. The festival lasts two days / three days / seven days.
2. There are about 100 bands / 200 bands / 1,000 bands.
3. The tickets cost from 80 to 180 euros / 180 to 515 euros / 180 to 550 euros.
4. More than 7,000 fans / 17,000 fans / 70,000 fans come to see the bands.
5. The cleaners look after 1,700 toilets / 1,800 toilets / 1,900 toilets.

3 Tutorial Seite 11

V 3
A5

c) Complete the sentences. Who does what?
Vervollständigen Sie die Sätze. Wer macht was?

electrician | personal assistant | waitress

1. *An electrician* repairs the lighting system in a house.
2. *A waitress* brings food and drinks to guests.
3. *A personal assistant* works in an office.
4. *A waitress* takes orders.
5. *An electrician* installs security cameras.
6. *A personal assistant* makes phone calls and writes e-mails.

Let's practise Seite 16

d) Choose two more sentences for the dialogue.
Wählen Sie zwei weitere Sätze aus, die zum Dialog passen.

[9] Yes, we swim indoors but I love going to the beach, too.
[ ] Oh what a pity. I love visiting the family.
[8] Really? But you can do a lot of fun things when it rains. Do you go swimming?
[ ] Are you sure there are no rainy days in Wales?

Unit 2

3 Reading Seite 21

d) Finish the sentences. Underline the correct word: **can, must, should** or **don't have to.**
*Vervollständigen Sie die Sätze. Unterstreichen Sie das richtige Wort: **can, must, should** oder **don't have to.***

1. You must / don't have to pay €450 a month for Flat A.
2. You can / must use a wheelchair in Flat C.
3. You can / don't have to have a car for House B.
4. House B is unfurnished. You should / can bring your own furniture.
5. You should / don't have to drive far to the city from Flat C.

1 Tutorial Seite 23

V 4 A 12 **f)** Complete the sentences with the words in the boxes.
Vervollständigen Sie die Sätze mit den Wörtern in den Kästchen.

doesn't cook | doesn't cost | don't know | don't want | doesn't drive

1. A room in a shared flat *doesn't cost* as much as a house.
2. I *don't know* much about Australia.
3. Benjamin loves his car but he *doesn't drive* to work.
4. Rebecca: "I like towns and I *don't want* to live in the country."
5. Benjamin washes up but he *doesn't cook* .

2 Tutorial Seite 24

V 5 A 13 **c)** Underline the correct answer.
Unterstreichen Sie die richtige Antwort.

1. The room costs £200 / £250 / £300 a month.
2. We pay £15 / £50 / £55 for heating, electricity and Wi-Fi.
3. We all give £12 / £20 / £22 for food for our cooking nights.
4. Benjamin earns £500 / £600 / £650 a month.

Unit 3

2 Listening Seite 33

A 19 **c)** Complete the sentences with the following words.
Vervollständigen Sie die Sätze mit den folgenden Wörtern.

hostel | children | couch | babysitter | people | outside

1. An au pair takes care of the *children* of a family.
2. If you want to work as an au pair you need to have some experience as a *babysitter* .
3. If you want to work on a farm you don't need money for a *hostel* .
4. You need to be fit and like working *outside* .
5. Your hosts will let you sleep on their *couch* .
6. You can travel like Hannah if you like meeting new *people* .

2 Listening Seite 34

e) Look at the offers on page 34 and make comparisons using the following words.
Schauen Sie sich die Angebote auf Seite 34 an und bilden Sie Vergleiche mit den folgenden Wörtern.

bigger than | longer than | as big as | more expensive than

The salary for Position B is bigger than the salary for Position A.

Job B lasts longer than Job A.

The host family in Position A is as big as the host family in Position B.

The flight for Position A is more expensive than for Position B.

2 Tutorial Seite 37

A 22 **a)** Listen to the phone call and fill in the correct information. Use the words in the boxes.
Hören Sie sich das Telefongespräch an und tragen Sie die richtigen Informationen ein. Folgende Wörter können Sie in das Online-Formular eintragen.

5 p.m. | Mary | 747 and 51 | 34 A | 10 to 13 April | McHenry Street

1. Name of host: *Mary*
2. Date of Andrew's visit: *10 to 13 April*
3. Time of arrival: *5 p.m.*
4. Bus numbers: *747 and 51*
5. Street name: *McHenry Street*
6. Flat number: *34 A*

Unit 4

2 Listening Seite 47

A 27 **b)** Listen to what Mike, Anna and Tom tell you about their jobs. Find out which qualities they need and complete the text with the following words.
Hören Sie sich an, was Mike, Anna und Tom Ihnen über ihre Jobs erzählen. Finden Sie heraus, welche Eigenschaften die drei brauchen und vervollständigen Sie den Text mit den folgenden Wörtern.

comfort | with machines | a team | children | creative | patient | work hard | quick | his hands | games | outside | food | hard-working | caring

1. Mike likes being *outside*. Sometimes he has to *work hard*. He likes working with *his hands* and is good at working *with machines*.
2. Anna loves spending time with *children*. She is *patient* and *caring*.
   She enjoys playing *games* with the kids but she also has to *comfort* the children when they are sick.
3. Tom loves working with *food* and being *creative*. As a cook he needs to be *quick* and *hard-working*.
   He also needs to be able to work in *a team*.

Unit 5

2 Listening Seite 61

A 38 **b)** Complete the sentences about Jenny. Use the words in the boxes.
Vervollständigen Sie die Sätze über Jenny. Verwenden Sie die Wörter in den Kästchen.

office | assistant | English | phone | skills | experience

1. Jenny is training to be a team *assistant* with a company that organizes events.
2. She got the addresses of companies from her local employment *office*.
3. With the help of a friend Jenny wrote a list of her *skills*.
4. Her work *experience* at the exhibition hall looked good in her CV.
5. Jenny wrote an *English* application and a CV.
6. She had to do a *phone* interview with *GoGlobal Fairs*.

1 Tutorial Seite 64

V 10
A 40

d) Think of more interview tips. You can also use the ideas in the box.
Überlegen Sie sich weitere Tipps für ein Jobinterview. Sie können auch die Wörter in den Kästchen verwenden.

check your phone | answer in complete sentences | smoke | be friendly | ~~chew gum~~ | thank the interviewer

DOS	DON'TS
Be friendly.	Example: *Don't chew gum.*
Thank the interviewer.	*Don't smoke.*
Answer in complete sentences.	*Don't check your phone.*

to chew *kauen* – **gum** *Kaugummi*

Jobsite Seite 66

b) Match the two parts of the sentences.
Verbinden Sie die zwei Satzhälften.

1. A trainee hairdresser also learns
2. The training course lasts
3. The trainee has to pay
4. The course takes place
5. A make-up artist learns
6. A make-up artist meets

a) € 650 a month.
b) to photoshop pictures as well.
c) one and a half years.
d) famous models.
e) to put on make-up.
f) on Mondays and Thursdays from 6 to 9 p.m.

Let's practise Seite 71

c) *Beantworten Sie die Fragen in ganzen Sätzen.*

1. Was macht Jenny im Moment? *Sie besucht einen Wirtschaftskurs an einem Berufskolleg.*
2. Warum will sie ihre Ausbildung bei *GoGlobal Fairs* machen?
   GoGlobal Fairs ist eine interessante Firma. Sie organisieren Events auf der ganzen Welt und bieten ein gutes Ausbildungsprogramm.
3. Nennen Sie drei von Jennys Fähigkeiten.
   Sie ist gut organisiert, gut in Sprachen und ist bereit, viel zu arbeiten.
4. Nennen Sie die Frage, die Jenny stellt. *Wann fängt der Job an?*
5. Wann wird Herr Malone zurückrufen? *Er wird in zwei Wochen zurückrufen.*

Unit 6

Your turn Seite 81

Schritt 3: Mit einem Partner / einer Partnerin wählen Sie eine Lösung *(solution)* aus. Verwenden Sie die Sätze im „You say"-Kästchen.

Solutions
- get a later bus
- send yourself a text message when it's time to clean your workbench
- talk to your boss / mum
- work fewer hours on Saturdays
- wear a shirt with long sleeves *(Ärmel)*

You say …

I think you should …
Why don't you …?
You could …
The best thing to do is to …

Let's practise Seite 83

A 54 **e)** *Hören Sie das Gespräch zwischen Sven und seinem Chef. Kreuzen Sie an: richtig oder falsch?*

	richtig	falsch
1. Mr Blair freut sich, weil Sven pünktlich zur Arbeit kommt.	X	
2. Sven kommt gerne rechtzeitig, um nicht den ganzen Tag müde zu sein.		X
3. Das Praktikum gefällt Sven nicht so gut.		X
4. Sven findet, dass in England manches anders ist, als er es erwartet hat.	X	
5. Sven erklärt, dass er viel arbeitet.		X
6. Mr Blair findet, dass Sven gut organisiert ist und gut im Team arbeitet.	X	
7. Sven wird in Zukunft versuchen, zu den Kunden direkter zu sein.		X
8. Mr Blair ist der Meinung, dass Sven gut Probleme lösen kann.	X	

G1 Sagen, was jemand gerne/nicht gerne mag oder tut

1 **So können Sie ausdrücken, ob jemand etwas mag oder nicht mag (*simple present*):**

I **like** sports.	*Ich **mag** Sport.*
Tom **loves** live music.	*Tom **liebt** Livemusik.*
Sarah **doesn't like** hard rock.	*Sarah **mag keinen** Hardrock.*
They **don't like** camping.	*Sie campen **nicht gerne**.*
We **enjoy** festivals.	*Uns **gefallen** (wörtlich: wir genießen) Festivals.*

2 **So können Sie ausdrücken, dass jemand etwas gerne oder nicht gerne tut (*gerund*):**

I **love** playing football.	*Ich spiele **gerne** Fußball.*
I **don't** like cooking.	*Ich koche **nicht gerne**.*
I **like** chatting with my friends.	*Ich chatte **gerne** mit meinen Freunden.*

Das Gerundium darf man nicht mit dem *present progressive* verwechseln:
I'm playing football. *Ich spiele gerade Fußball.* / I **love playing** football. *Ich spiele gerne Fußball.*

Sie können auch sagen:
Playing football is my favourite sport. / ***Fußball** ist mein Lieblingssport.*

a) Vervollständigen Sie die Sätze mit Dingen oder Aktivitäten, die Sie gerne oder nicht gerne mögen.

1. I like *meeting new people and I also like* ______
2. I love ______
3. I don't like ______
4. I hate ______

b) Vervollständigen Sie die Sätze mit **like** ☺, **don't/ doesn't like** ☹ und **love** ♥.

1. Emily *doesn't like* ☹ free climbing.
2. Andrew *loves* ♥ heavy metal.
3. Finn and Anna *like* ☺ going to festivals.
4. Sarah *loves* ♥ her new sunglasses.
5. My friends and I *don't like* ☹ going camping.
6. I *love* ☺ the new food truck in our park!

● c) Bringen Sie die Wörter in die richtige Reihenfolge.

1. with / is / friends / cooking / fun — *Cooking with friends is fun.*
2. music / is / going / to / festivals / of / fun / a lot — *Going to music festivals is a lot of fun.*
3. meeting / is / people / new / interesting — *Meeting new people is interesting.*
4. necessary / is / often / working / Saturdays / on — *Working on Saturdays is often necessary.*
5. sun / great / is / spending / a / in / the / holiday — *Spending a holiday in the sun is great.*
6. family / holidays / is / visiting / boring / on / my — *Visiting family on my holidays is boring.*

G2 Sagen, wie etwas ist oder was regelmäßig geschieht

1 So können Sie ausdrücken, was jemand immer oder regelmäßig macht/nicht macht (*simple present*):

I get up at 6:30 **every day.**	*Ich stehe* ***jeden*** *Tag um 6:30 Uhr auf.*
You **usually** start work at 8:00.	*Du fängst* ***gewöhnlich*** *um 8 Uhr mit der Arbeit an.*
We **often** have breakfast on Sundays at 10:00.	*Wir frühstücken sonntags* ***oft*** *um 10 Uhr.*
I **don't have** breakfast every morning.	*Ich* ***frühstücke nicht*** *jeden Tag.*
My girlfriend **doesn't drink** tea for breakfast.	*Meine Freundin* ***trinkt keinen*** *Tee zum Frühstück.*
I **sometimes** go jogging, but I **never** go dancing.	*Ich gehe* ***manchmal*** *joggen, aber ich gehe* ***nie*** *tanzen.*

Denken Sie daran:
He **starts** work at 8:30 a.m. / He **doesn't start** work at 10:00 a.m.
She **cooks** dinner on Sundays. / She **doesn't cook** dinner on Mondays.

Signalwörter:
always *immer* / usually *gewöhnlich* / often *oft* / sometimes *manchmal* / never *nie* / on Mondays *montags* / every day *täglich*

2 So können Sie Fragen stellen:

Do you **live** at home?	***Wohnst*** *du zu Hause?*
Does Jannik **live** in a shared flat?	***Wohnt*** *Jannik in einer WG?*
Where **do** you **work**?	*Wo* ***arbeitest*** *du?*
When **does** work **start**?	*Wann* ***fängt*** *die Arbeit* ***an****?*

Fragewörter: what *was/wie* / when *wann* / where *wo* / who *wer* / why *warum* / how *wie*

3 So können Sie sagen und fragen, wie etwas ist (*to be*):

Are you from Australia?	***Kommst*** *du aus Australien?*
Is it far to the bus stop?	***Ist*** *die Bushaltestelle weit weg?*

a) Ergänzen Sie die richtige Verbform.

1. Jenny *goes* (go) shopping after work.
2. William: "I *work* (work) for a big company in London."
3. Jane often *has* (have) lunch in the cafeteria.
4. Sam *does* (do) the housework at the weekend.
5. Nick and David *finish* (finish) work at 6 p.m.
6. We *play* (play) football on Saturdays.

b) Schreiben Sie ganze Sätze.

1. to work / usually / I / drive — *I usually drive to work.*
2. takes / Andrew / the bus / never — *Andrew never takes the bus.*
3. always / her / emails / checks / Rebecca — *Rebecca always checks her emails.*
4. organizes / sometimes / Ashling / meetings — *Ashling sometimes organizes meetings.*
5. often / phone calls / we / in the mornings / make — *We often make phone calls in the mornings.*

c) Vervollständigen Sie die Sätze.

1. We work from Monday to Friday. We *don't work* (not work) on Saturday.
2. Jannik lives at home. He *doesn't live* (not live) in a shared flat.
3. The flat costs £500 a month. It *doesn't cost* (not cost) £1,000 a month.
4. Rebecca and Andrew get up at 7 a.m. They *don't get up* (not get up) at 6 a.m.
5. I want to find a room in a shared flat. I *don't want* (not want) to live alone.

d) Vervollständigen Sie den Lückentext mit den richtigen Fragen.

E-MAIL

Hey Sophia,

It's great that you and Luke have a nice, new home together on the water.

How far *do you travel* (you / travel) to work? *Does Luke* (Luke / travel) to Greenwich every day?

How much rent *do you and Luke pay* (you and Luke / pay) a month? *Does Luke help* (Luke / help) with the housework? Who *do you live* (you / live) next to?

Where *do you park* (you / park) the boat at night?

As you can see I have lots of questions. When *do you have time* (you / have) time for a visitor?

I really want to see you and the boat!

Write soon.
Love Katy

G3 Sagen, was jemand machen kann, muss oder soll

1 **So können Sie ausdrücken, was jemand machen kann/nicht machen kann (*can/can't*):**

Can I help you with the housework?	***Kann*** *ich dir mit der Hausarbeit helfen?*
You **can't** move into the flat until April.	*Sie **können nicht** vor April einziehen.*

Culture Tip
In englischsprachigen Ländern wird sehr viel Wert auf Höflichkeit gelegt:
Could you help me with the housework, please?
Könntest du mir bitte bei der Hausarbeit helfen?

2 **So können Sie ausdrücken, was jemand tun muss/nicht tun muss (*must/don't have to*):**

I **have to** pay € 500 a month for rent.	*Ich **muss** monatlich 500 € Miete zahlen.*
We **don't have to** pay rent.	*Wir **müssen keine** Miete zahlen.*
You **have to** bring your own furniture.	*Sie **müssen** Ihre eigenen Möbel mitbringen.*
He **doesn't have to** bring his own furniture.	*Er **muss keine** eigenen Möbel mitbringen.*

Achtung:
Mustn't = nicht dürfen / Statt **have to/has to** können Sie auch **must** verwenden

3 So können Sie ausdrücken, was jemand tun soll/nicht tun soll (*should/shouldn't*):

The flat **should** be near work.	*Die Wohnung **soll** in der Nähe der Arbeit sein.*
The flat **shouldn't** be too expensive.	*Die Wohnung **soll** nicht zu teuer sein.*

Beachten Sie:
Mit **should/shouldn't** können Sie auch Ratschläge erteilen:
It's hot – You **should** drink water. / On your first day at work you **shouldn't** be late.

a) Vervollständigen Sie die Sätze mit ***can*** oder ***can't***.

1. I don't know if I _can_ finish the work on time.
2. _Can_ you help me to find my phone?
3. I'm sorry I _can't_ help you. I'm too busy at the moment.
4. _Can_ I close the window? It's really cold in here.
5. Our assistants _can't_ open the shop. They don't have a key.
6. The flat is very expensive. I _can't_ afford to move in.

b) Vervollständigen Sie die Sätze mit **have to / has to** oder **don't have to / doesn't have to.**

1. Ben: "I _have to_ get up at 6 o'clock every morning."
2. Ben sometimes _has to_ work night shifts.
3. Ben _doesn't have to_ cook for the others every day.
4. Rebecca and Andrew _don't have to_ work on Sundays.
5. Tim McMahon: "We want a place in the Cork area, but we _have to_ sell our house first."
6. Tomorrow is Saturday so I _don't have to_ get up for work.

c) Vervollständigen Sie die Sätze mit **should** oder **shouldn't**.

1. I'm tired. – Well, you _shouldn't_ work so much.
2. We always do the housework. You really _should_ help us sometimes.
3. I think you _should_ spend less money on clothes.
4. You _shouldn't_ drink so much coffee every day.
5. Do you think Simon _should_ look for a job as a team assistant?
6. I think that you _shouldn't_ always do your homework at the last minute!

G4 Sagen, was in der Vergangenheit war oder passiert ist

1 So können Sie ausdrücken, was in der Vergangenheit passiert/nicht passiert ist (*simple past*):

I play**ed** football yesterday.	*Ich **habe** gestern Fußball **gespielt**.*
We visit**ed** friends in London last week.	*Letzte Woche **haben** wir Freunde in London **besucht**.*
I **didn't go** to school yesterday.	*Ich **bin** gestern nicht zur Schule **gegangen**.*
Tom and Luke **didn't like** the hostel in Belfast.	*Tom und Luke **haben** das Hostel in Belfast **nicht gemocht**.*

Beachten Sie: Manche Verben sind unregelmäßig: do → did / have → had / go → went
Diese sollten Sie auswendig lernen. Eine Liste der unregelmäßigen Verben finden Sie auf S. 100–101.

Signalwörter: yesterday *gestern* / last year *letztes Jahr* / last week *letzte Woche* / in 2015 *im Jahr 2015*

Im Deutschen gibt es verschiedene Möglichkeiten das *simple present* zu übersetzen:
Tim met Sarah. → *Tim **traf** Sarah. / Tim **hat** Sarah **getroffen**.*

2 So können Sie ausdrücken, was in der Vergangenheit war/nicht war (*to be*):

I **wasn't** at home last night, I **was** in the cinema.	*Ich **war** gestern Abend **nicht** zu Hause, ich **war** im Kino.*
We **weren't** at work, we **were** at school.	*Wir **waren nicht** auf der Arbeit, wir **waren** in der Schule.*

3 So können Sie Fragen stellen:

Did you **stay** at a hostel?	***Hast** du in einem Hostel **übernachtet**?*
Did Ben **work** on a farm?	***Hat** Ben auf einer Farm **gearbeitet**?*
Where **did** you **work**?	*Wo **hast** du **gearbeitet**?*
When **did** work **start**?	*Wann **hat** die Arbeit **angefangen**?*

a) Vervollständigen Sie die folgenden Sätze.

1. Last week I *invited* (invite) Sarah to my party.
2. My mum *didn't call* (not call) me.
3. The boys *didn't go* (not go) home.
4. I really *liked* (like) the band last night.
5. I *wanted* (want) to visit Tim but he *wasn't* (not be) at home.

● b) Übersetzen Sie die folgenden Sätze ins Englische.

1. Lisa arbeitete ein Jahr lang als Au-pair.

Lisa worked as an au pair for a year.

2. Luke reiste durch Australien.

Luke travelled through Australia.

3. Luke brauchte kein Geld für Jugendherbergen.

Luke didn't need money for hostels.

4. Hannahs Gastgeber zeigten ihr die Sehenswürdigkeiten.

Hannah's hosts showed her the sights.

c) Vervollständigen Sie die unregelmäßigen Verben.

meet – *met* wear – *wore* become – *became* hear – *heard* lose – *lost* say – *said*

G5 So vergleichen Sie Personen oder Sachen

So vergleichen Sie Personen und Sachen (*comparison of adjectives*):

Philip is **older than** Sarah.	*Philip ist **älter als** Sarah.*
Berlin **is bigger than** Stuttgart.	*Berlin ist **größer als** Stuttgart.*
Italy is **hotter than** Ireland.	*In Italien ist es **wärmer als** in Irland.*
English is **easier than** maths.	*Englisch ist **einfacher als** Mathe.*
Australia is **more interesting** than England.	*Australien ist **interessanter** als England.*
The Queen is **more famous** than Camilla.	*Die Queen ist **berühmter** als Camilla.*

Beachten Sie:
Bei einsilbigen Adjektiven hängt man ein *-er* an: old – old**er**
Endet das Adjektiv auf **-t** oder **-g**, so wird der Buchstabe verdoppelt: big – big**ger** / hot – hot**ter**
Auch bei zweisilbigen Adjektiven, die auf **-er**, **-le**, **-y** oder **-ow** enden, hängt man ein **-er** an.
Bei Adjektiven, die auf **-y** enden, wird das **y** zu **-ier**: eas**y** – eas**ier** / happ**y** – happ**ier**

Mehrsilbige Adjektive werden mit *more* gesteigert: interesting – **more** interesting

a) Vervollständigen Sie die folgenden Sätze mit einem Vergleich.

1. A mouse is *smaller than* (small) a cat.
2. Spain is *hotter than* (hot) England.
3. I think hockey is *more interesting than* (interesting) football.
4. Sarah is *prettier than* (pretty) Ashley.
5. My plane leaves *earlier than* (early) your plane.
6. New York is *more exciting than* (exciting) my home town.

● **b)** Übersetzen Sie die folgenden Sätze ins Englische.

1. Ein Hostel ist billiger als ein Hotel.
   A hostel is cheaper than a hotel.
2. Berlin ist größer als Stuttgart.
   Berlin is bigger than Stuttgart.
3. Ein Tiger ist gefährlicher als eine Katze.
   A tiger is more dangerous than a cat.
4. England ist kälter als Italien.
   England is colder than Italy.
5. Nate ist glücklicher als Tim.
   Nate is happier than Tim.
6. London ist teurer als York.
   London is more expensive than York.

G6 Sagen, was jetzt gerade passiert

1 **So sagen Sie, was jetzt gerade oder zurzeit passiert/oder nicht passiert (*present progressive*):**

She **is taking** the children to kindergarten right now.	*Sie **bringt** die Kinder gerade in den Kindergarten.*
I **am picking** apples today.	*Ich **pflücke** heute Äpfel.*
They **are relaxing** after work in this photo.	*Auf diesem Foto **erholen** sie sich von der Arbeit.*
I **am not ('m not) looking** for a hotel in the country.	*Ich **suche** nicht nach einem Hotel auf dem Land.*
He **is not (isn't) working** today.	*Er **arbeitet** heute **nicht**.*
They **are not (aren't) having** a couch surfing guest.	*Sie **haben keinen** Couchsurfing-Gast.*

Beachten Sie:
Gesprochen werden meist die Kurzformen:
I am → I'm / you are → you're / she is → she's / we are → we're / they are → they're

Signalwörter: now *jetzt/nun* / just *gerade* / at the moment *im Moment*

2 **So können Sie Fragen stellen:**

Are you **preparing** a snack?	***Bereitest** du **gerade** einen Snack zu?*
Is Ben **repairing** his bike?	***Repariert** Ben **gerade** sein Fahrrad?*
What **are** you **doing**?	*Was **machst** du **gerade**?*

a) Vervollständigen Sie die folgenden Sätze.

1. Sarah *is working* (work) at the Dublin City Hostel this summer.
2. John and Andrew *are planning* (plan) to do couch surfing on their holiday.
3. Jacob *isn't repairing* (not repair) the tractor today. He has a day off.
4. I *am making* (make) breakfast for the children at the moment.
5. Luke and his friends *aren't working* (not work) this week.
6. They *are sightseeing* (sightsee) in Sydney.

● b) Übersetzen Sie die folgenden Sätze ins Englische.

1. Emma trifft gerade ihre Gastgeber.

Emma is meeting her hosts.

2. Jacob pflückt gerade Äpfel.

Jacob is picking apples.

3. Die Kinder machen gerade keine Hausaufgaben.

The kids aren't doing their homework.

4. Andrew und Ben spielen gerade Fußball.

Andrew and Ben are playing football.

5. Rebecca arbeitet heute nicht.

Rebecca isn't working today.

6. Emily und Rebecca schauen sich gerade Jobanzeigen an.

Emily and Rebecca are looking at job adverts.

G7 So reden Sie über spontane Entscheidungen/Vermutungen

So können Sie Vermutungen oder spontane Entscheidungen ausdrücken (*will-future*):

Oh, there is Sarah – I **will go** over and say hi.	*Oh, da ist Sarah – ich **werde** kurz rübergehen und „hi" sagen.*
I think Tom **will call** me tomorrow.	*Ich denke, Tom **wird** mich morgen anrufen.*
I hope it **won't** rain next week.	*Ich hoffe, es **wird** nächste Woche nicht regnen.*
Do you think we **will** see a wombat?	*Denkst du, dass wir einen Wombat **sehen werden**?*

Beachten Sie:
Gesprochen werden meist die Kurzformen:
I'**ll** go shopping tomorrow. I think they'**ll** visit us later.
Achtung!
Will sollten Sie nicht mit **want to** verwechseln:
I **will buy** some souvenirs. *Ich **werde** ein paar Souvenirs kaufen.*
I **want to buy** some souvenirs. *Ich **möchte** ein paar Souvenirs kaufen.*

Signalwörter:
maybe *vielleicht* / I think *ich denke* / I hope *ich hoffe*

Im Deutschen gibt es verschiedene Möglichkeiten, Sätze im *will-future* zu übersetzen.
We **will** wait for you. → *Wir **werden** auf dich warten. / Wir **warten** auf dich.*

a) Bilden Sie die korrekte Verbform.

1. I'm hungry, I think I *will have* (have) a little snack.
2. It has just stopped raining so we *will go* (go) to the park with my dog.
3. My teacher has just called to say he's sick so there *won't be* (not be) any piano lessons today.
4. Anna looks very unhappy. I *will go* (go) over and talk to her.
5. I don't think the sun *will shine* (shine) tomorrow.
6. You've studied a lot, so I think you *won't have* (not have) any problems in the exam.

● **b)** Übersetzen Sie die folgenden Sätze.

1. Ich glaube, Andrews Flugzeug wird um 14 Uhr ankommen.

I think Andrew's plane will arrive at 2 p.m.

2. Vielleicht besuche ich nach der Schule meine Freundin.

Maybe I will visit my girlfriend after school.

3. „Ich habe mein Geld vergessen."– „Kein Problem, ich werde für dich bezahlen!"

"I have forgotten my money." – "No problem, I will pay for you!"

4. Keine Sorge, es wird nicht lange dauern.

Don't worry, it won't take long.

5. Ich denke, wir werden morgen ins Kino gehen.

I think we'll go to the cinema tomorrow.

6. Ich bin sehr müde. Ich werde jetzt mit der Arbeit aufhören.

I'm really tired. I'll finish work now.

G8 Sagen, was unter bestimmten Bedingungen passieren wird

So können Sie ausdrücken, was unter einer bestimmten Bedingung passieren wird (*if-clauses*):

Mike **will work** outside **if he gets** a job on a farm.	***Wenn*** *Mike einen Job auf einem Bauernhof bekommt,* ***wird*** *er draußen arbeiten.*
Tom **won't work** outside **if he gets** a job as a cook.	*Tom* ***wird nicht*** *draußen arbeiten,* ***wenn*** *er einen Job als Koch bekommt.*
If it's too dark, I **won't take** any photos.	***Wenn*** *es zu dunkel ist,* ***mache*** *ich keine Fotos.*

Beachten Sie: Wenn die „if-Sätze" mit einem Hauptsatz beginnen, entfällt das Komma.
I'll be unhappy if you don't come to my party. / If you don't come to my party, I'll be unhappy.

a) Bilden Sie die richtige Verbform.

1. You *will need* (need) to be good at languages if you work as a tour guide.
2. If you work as a customer service agent, you *will have to* (have to) be polite and organized.
3. Jake will need to be fit if he *gets* (get) a summer job in a brewery.
4. The youth club *won't give* (not give) you a job if you aren't patient with children.
5. If you *work* (work) on our farm, you will learn about organic farming.
6. If you *don't have* (not have) experience, we won't give you the job.

G9 Über etwas sprechen, das angefangen hat, aber noch nicht zu Ende ist

1 **So können Sie über etwas sprechen, das in der Vergangenheit begonnen hat und bis zum heutigen Tag andauert (*present perfect*):**

Jenny works at *GoGlobal Fairs*. She **has done** a lot of different things there.	*Jenny arbeitet bei* GoGlobal Fairs. *Sie* ***hat*** *dort bereits viele unterschiedliche Dinge* ***gemacht****.*
We are at a music festival. We **have met** some interesting people.	*Wir sind auf einem Musik-Festival. Wir* ***haben*** *schon einige interessante Leute* ***kennengelernt****.*
Simon **has written** a lot of applications this month.	*Simon* ***hat*** *in diesem Monat viele Bewerbungen* ***geschrieben****.*
We **have done** a yoga course this summer.	*Wir* ***haben*** *diesen Sommer einen Yoga-Kurs* ***gemacht****.*

Beachten Sie: Die Verbform wird mit *have/has* und der dritten Form des Verbs gebildet. Sie finden eine Liste der unregelmäßigen dritten Verbformen auf Seite 100 – 101.

Signalwörter: already *schon* / just *gerade* / ever *jemals (in Fragen)*

2 **So können Sie den Zeitpunkt in der Vergangenheit festlegen:**

I have worked as a team assistant **since** January.	*Ich arbeite* ***seit Januar*** *als Teamassistentin.*
He has worked as a team assistant **for** six months.	*Er arbeitet* ***seit sechs Monaten*** *als Teamassistent.*

Beachten Sie:
Since verwenden Sie in Zusammenhang mit einem bestimmten Zeit**punkt** (*since 2017, since my birthday, since April*). *For* verwenden Sie für einen Zeit**raum** (*for one year, for a month, for a long time*).

a) Bilden Sie die richtige Verbform. → Irregular verbs, pages 100–101

1. Ben has helped (help) me with my applications this week.
2. Andrew has an interview today so he has checked (check) his letter of application again.
3. Andrew hasn't turned off (not turn off) his phone.
4. Rebecca has made (make) a good impression at the interview.
5. Jenny hasn't got (not get) a job in a hospital.
6. Simon hasn't done (not do) many job interviews.

b) Ergänzen Sie die Sätze mit *for* oder *since*.

1. Patrick has worked for *GoGlobal Fairs* since February.
2. I haven't seen my best friend since she went to Australia last year.
3. Andrew has worked as a bike courier for six months.
4. Rebecca has changed her outfit three times since she got up this morning.
5. Emily has trained the football team for two years.
6. Jenny has only worked for *GoGlobal Fairs* for a very short time.

G10 Sagen oder fragen, was man / jemand in der Zukunft vorhat

1 So kann man über seine Pläne für die Zukunft sprechen:

I'm **going to be** a waitress. My brother **is going to visit** me next weekend.	*Ich **habe vor**, Kellnerin zu werden.* *Mein Bruder **wird** mich nächstes Wochenende **besuchen**.*

2 Sie verwenden *going to* und das Verb:

Elsa and Ole **are going to meet** their German friend later.	*Elsa und Ole **haben vor**, ihre deutsche Freundin später zu treffen.*

3 Wenn Sie vorhaben, etwas nicht zu tun, verwenden Sie die Verneinung von *to be + going to:*

We **aren't going to work** in the holidays.	*Wir **haben nicht vor**, in den Ferien zu arbeiten.*

4 Wenn Sie jemanden nach seinen Plänen fragen, verwenden Sie die Frageform von *to be + going to:*

Are you **going to do** an English course?	***Wirst** du einen Englischkurs **machen**?*

a) Vervollständigen Sie die Sätze.

1. Tim has found a new job. He 's going to work (work) in a call centre.
2. Sam and Nick are going to travel (travel) in the USA next summer.
3. When you start college, you 're going to meet (meet) a lot of new people!
4. I want to leave England. I 'm going to go (go) to Canada and work there.
5. Nancy is going to be (be) a gardener when she's 16.

b) Bringen Sie die Wörter in die richtige Reihenfolge. Achtung: Die Verbformen sind alle verneint.

1. a / isn't / work / going to / in / Tim / hotel — Tim isn't going to work in a hotel.
2. hotel room / aren't / our / going to / We / complain about — We aren't going to complain about our hotel room.
3. not going / I'm / my desk / time / to have / to clean — I'm not going to have time to clean my desk.
4. going / at college / My friends / aren't / to stay — My friends aren't going to stay at college.
5. aren't / Ron and Evan / going / anymore / to smoke — Ron and Evan aren't going to smoke anymore.

c) Bilden Sie Fragen mit *going to*. Fragen Sie nach den unterstrichenen Wörtern.

1. I'm going to do <u>an apprenticeship</u> after school. — What are you going to do after school?
2. Kristin is going to wear <u>a uniform</u> in her job. — What is Kristin going to wear in her job?
3. <u>Trudi</u> is going to help me with my applications. — Who is going to help you?
4. Ben is going to work <u>in a hotel</u> in the summer. — Where is Ben going to work?
5. Jack is going to get an earlier bus <u>because he was late yesterday</u>. — Why is Jack going to get an earlier bus?
6. Pete and Jenny are going to apply for jobs <u>after college</u>. — When are Pete and Jenny going to apply for jobs?

Irregular verbs

Infinitive	Simple past	Past participle	Deutsch
to be	was / were	been	*sein*
to become	became	become	*werden*
to begin	began	begun	*anfangen, beginnen*
to break	broke	broken	*brechen, kaputt machen*
to bring	brought	brought	*bringen*
to buy	bought	bought	*kaufen*
can	could	–	*können*
to catch	caught	caught	*fangen*
to come	came	come	*kommen*
to cost	cost	cost	*kosten*
to cut	cut	cut	*schneiden*
to deal with	dealt	dealt	*umgehen mit*
to do	did	done	*machen, tun*
to drink	drank	drunk	*trinken*
to drive	drove	driven	*fahren*
to eat	ate	eaten	*essen*
to fall	fell	fallen	*fallen*
to feel	felt	felt	*fühlen, sich fühlen*
to find	found	found	*finden*
to forget	forgot	forgotten	*vergessen*
to get	got	got	*bekommen, erhalten, werden*
to give	gave	given	*geben*
to go	went	gone	*gehen, fahren*
to grow	grew	grown	*wachsen*
to hang out	hung	hung	*abhängen, sich herumtreiben*
to have (got)	had	had	*haben*
to hear	heard	heard	*hören*
to hurt	hurt	hurt	*wehtun*
to keep	kept	kept	*behalten, aufbewahren*
to know	knew	known	*wissen, kennen*
to let	let	let	*lassen*
to lie	lay	lain	*liegen, sich hinlegen*
to make	made	made	*machen*
to mean	meant	meant	*meinen, bedeuten*
to meet	met	met	*treffen, kennenlernen*
to pay	paid	paid	*zahlen, bezahlen*
to put	put	put	*setzen, stellen, legen*
to read	read	read	*lesen*
to ride	rode	ridden	*reiten, fahren*
to ring	rang	rung	*klingeln, anrufen*
to run	ran	run	*laufen, rennen*
to say	said	said	*sagen*
to see	saw	seen	*sehen*
to sell	sold	sold	*verkaufen*
to send	sent	sent	*schicken, senden*
to show	showed	shown	*zeigen*
to sing	sang	sung	*singen*

to sit	sat	sat	*sitzen*
to sleep	slept	slept	schlafen
to speak	spoke	spoken	*sprechen*
to spend	spent	spent	*verbringen, ausgeben*
to stand	stood	stood	*stehen*
to swim	swam	swum	*schwimmen*
to take	took	taken	*nehmen, brauchen, dauern*
to teach	taught	taught	*unterrichten*
to tell	told	told	*erzählen, sagen*
to think	thought	thought	*denken, glauben, meinen*
to understand	understood	understood	*verstehen*
to wake (up)	woke	woken	*aufwachen*
to wear	wore	worn	*tragen, anziehen*
to win	won	won	*gewinnen*
to write	wrote	written	*schreiben*

So können Sie Sätze mit den unregelmäßigen Verben bilden:

Simple present:	I **am** at college today.	*Heute **bin** ich im Berufskolleg.*
Simple past:	I **was** at college yesterday.	*Gestern **war** ich im Berufskolleg.*
Past participle:	I **have been** at college since September.	*Ich **bin** seit September auf dem Berufskolleg.*

Musterlösungen: Unit 3

2 Tutorial: How to talk on the phone → Seite 38

d) **Host:** Hello, Kate Fields speaking.
Guest: Hello Mrs Fields. This is … (your own name). I'm calling about your offer of a sofa.
Host: Yes, I can offer you a couch in our spare room. When would you like to come?
Guest: Great. I would like to stay with you from 8 to 10 March.
Host: That's fine.
Guest: How do I get to your place?
Host: You take the no. 12 bus from the airport to Oxford Street. Then you walk down Oxford Street. Our flat is at number 2 Oxford Street.
Guest: Great, thank you very much. I'm looking forward to meeting you.
Host: OK, see you soon! Take care, bye.
Guest: Bye.

Jobsite: Jacob's blog: Working on a farm → Seite 41

a) *Erstes Foto:* We planted, weeded and watered the crops. (Zeile 9)
Zweites Foto: In the autumn we were very busy picking apples … (Zeile 11)
Drittes Foto: I also had to work with farm machines like tractors … (Zeile 10)
Viertes Foto: We then sold the products at local farmer's markets and in a little shop on the farm. (Zeilen 12 –13)

So gehen Sie vor, wenn Sie ein Bild beschreiben möchten.

1. Sagen Sie, was für ein **Bild** es ist.

It's a photo!

It's a map.

2. Fassen Sie die Szene in **einem Satz** zusammen.

The picture shows …

3. Beschreiben Sie **Details** und sagen Sie, **wo** diese auf dem Foto zu finden sind.

in the foreground

in the background

on the left

on the right

4. Sagen Sie, was auf dem **Bild** passiert. Hierfür verwenden Sie immer die -ing Form.

z. B. A man is sitting at the table.

5. Beschreiben Sie Ihren eigenen **Eindruck**.

I think the people in the photo are happy.

So gehen Sie vor, wenn Sie einen Text verstehen möchten.

1. Lesen Sie die **Überschrift**. = heading

2. Ist ein **Foto** zum Text abgedruckt?

Schauen Sie was darauf zu sehen ist.

3. Überfliegen Sie den **Text**.

Unterstreichen Sie wichtige Schlagworte. = keywords

Um welches Thema geht es?

4. Lesen Sie den **ersten Abschnitt** = paragraph genau. Worum geht es?

Unterstreichen Sie wichtige Schlagworte.

5. Gehen Sie mit jedem Abschnitt = paragraph so vor wie in Schritt 4.

So verstehen Sie ein Tutorial.

1. Lesen Sie die Aufgabe zum Tutorial durch.
Was sollen Sie herausfinden?
Oft erhalten Sie Hinweise:
- **Wen** werden Sie sehen?
- **Worum** geht es?

2. Schauen Sie das Tutorial an.
Am Anfang wird immer erklärt, **was** Sie lernen werden.

3. Achten Sie auf Details:
Was machen und sagen die Personen?

4. Machen Sie sich **Notizen**, die beim Beantworten der Aufgabe helfen.
Vielleicht können Sie Teile der Aufgabe bereits beim Zuschauen bearbeiten.

5. Falls Sie das Tutorial **erneut anschauen**, achten Sie auf weitere Details und verbessern Sie Ihre Lösungen.

So lernen Sie Vokabeln.

1. **Sammeln** Sie **alle Vokabeln**, die für das Thema wichtig sind:
- aus Aufschrieben,
- aus dem Schulbuch,
- von Arbeitsblättern etc.

2. Notieren Sie direkt daneben die Übersetzung(en).

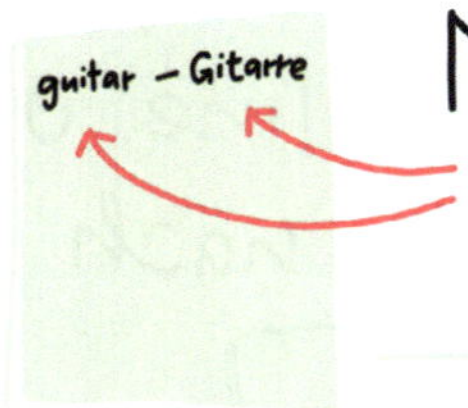

3. Es gibt viele Möglichkeiten, Vokabeln zu lernen, z.B.
- immer wieder aufschreiben, am besten per Hand
- lesen (still oder laut)
- auf das Smartphone sprechen und immer wieder anhören.

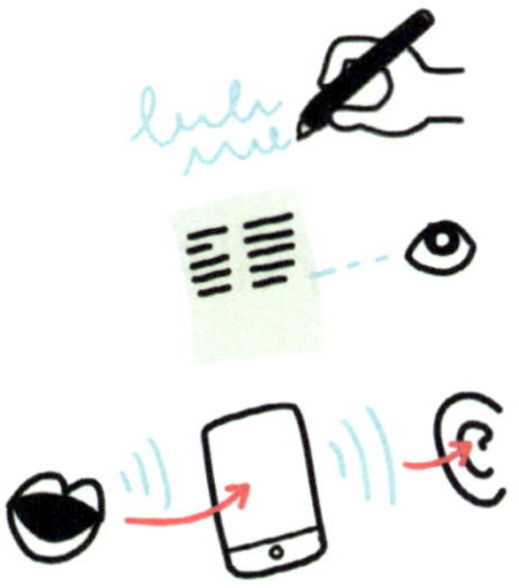

Finden Sie die Methode, die am besten zu Ihnen passt.

4. Üben Sie jeden Tag ca. **10 – 15 Wörter** – wenige Minuten genügen.

So gehen Sie mit unbekannten Wörtern um.

1. Schauen Sie zuerst, ob sich das Wort aus dem **Zusammenhang** im Text erklären lässt.

2. Falls nicht: schlagen Sie es im **Wörterbuch**, online oder in einer App nach.

3. ⚠ **ACHTUNG**: Viele Wörter haben mehrere Bedeutungen.

z.B. glasses → Brille
→ Gläser

4. Wenn Sie Verben nachschlagen, benötigen Sie die Grundform mit **„to"**

to wear → wore → worn

Infinitiv | Simple Past | Past Participle

So telefonieren Sie auf Englisch.

Vor dem Telefonat:

- Überlegen Sie, was Sie sagen möchten:
  Wie werden Sie die Person begrüßen? **Wie** stellen Sie sich vor?
- Machen Sie sich Notizen:
  Welche Fragen möchten Sie stellen?
  Welche Infos brauchen Sie?

Beim Telefonat:

- **Begrüßen** Sie die Person und sagen Sie, warum Sie anrufen.
- Fragen Sie nach, wenn Sie etwas nicht verstehen.
- **Notieren** Sie, was Ihnen Ihr/e Gesprächspartner/in sagt.
- Verabschieden Sie sich freundlich und bedanken Sie sich für das Gespräch.

So verstehen Sie einen Hörtext.

1. Lesen Sie die Aufgabe zum Hörtext durch.

- Welche Infos sollen Sie heraus finden?
- Oft erhalten Sie auch Hinweise: Welche **Personen** werden Sie gleich hören? Wie ist die **Situation**?

2. Achten Sie beim ersten Hören darauf, worum es geht.

- Wer ist beteiligt?
- Wo spielt es?

TIPP: Hintergrundgeräusche können Hinweise geben.

3. Machen Sie Notizen, die beim **Beantworten** helfen. Vielleicht können Sie Teile der Aufgabe bereits beim Anhören bearbeiten.

4. Falls Sie den Text erneut anhören, achten Sie auf **weitere Details**. Verbessern und ergänzen Sie Ihre Lösungen.

So meistern Sie Prüfungen

VORBEREITUNG

1. Machen Sie eine Liste der **Dinge**, die Sie lernen müssen.

Überlegen Sie, **was** Sie **wann** lernen.

2. Fangen Sie früh an und üben Sie **jeden Tag** ein wenig.

PRÜFUNGSSITUATION

3. Beantworten Sie als erstes die Fragen, die Ihnen **leicht** fallen. So haben Sie mehr Zeit für die **schwierigen** Aufgaben übrig.

4. Wenn etwas unklar ist, bitten Sie Ihren Lehrer, die **Aufgabe** zu erklären.

So machen Sie eine Mediation.

1. Lesen Sie die **Aufgabe** genau:
- An wen soll sich Ihre **Mediation** richten?
- In welcher **Form** (z. B. Email, Stichwörter) und Sprache?
- Welche **Infos** sind gefragt?

2. Lesen Sie den **Text** mehrmals.

Unbekannte Wörter können Sie nachschlagen.

3. Unterstreichen oder notieren Sie die Infos, die für die **Lösung** nötig sind.

4. Schreiben Sie nun Ihre **Mediation**: Bilden Sie kurze, einfache Sätze.

ACHTUNG: Machen Sie keine direkte Übersetzung!

5. Lesen Sie Ihre Mediation gründlich durch. Haben Sie alles aus Punkt 1 bedacht?

Alphabetical word list

A

abroad [ə'brɔ:d] im/ins Ausland Unit 3, 33
accident ['æksɪdnt] Unfall Unit 2, 21
accurate ['ækjərət] akkurat, genau Unit 4, 55
to **afford** [ə'fɔ:d] sich leisten Unit 2, 21
ago [ə'gəʊ] vor Unit 1, 8
amazing [ə'meɪzɪŋ] erstaunlich Unit 1, 8
angry ['æŋgri] verärgert Unit 6, 77
another [ə'nʌðə] ein(e) andere/-r/-s Unit 6, 73
apartment block [ə'pɑ:tmənt ˌblɒk] Mehrfamilienhaus Unit 2, 20
application [ˌæplɪ'keɪʃn] Bewerbung Unit 4, 51
to **apply for** [ə'plaɪ fə] sich bewerben um/für Unit 5, 60
apprenticeship [ə'prentɪʃɪp] Lehre, Ausbildung Unit 6, 76
assistant [ə'sɪstnt] Assistent/-in Unit 2, 26
at any time [ət‿eni 'taɪm] jederzeit Unit 5, 62
to **attend** [ə'tend] zur Verfügung stehen, teilnehmen Unit 5, 62
au pair [ˌəʊ'peə] Au-pair Unit 3, 32

B

backpack ['bækpæk] Rucksack Unit 3, 32
badly organized [ˌbædli‿'ɔ:gənaɪzd] schlecht organisiert Unit 6, 72
band [bænd] Musikband Unit 1, 7
*to **be in a hurry** [bi‿ɪn‿ə 'hʌri] es eilig haben Unit 6, 73
*to **be stuck** [ˌbi 'stʌk] hängenbleiben Unit 6, 74
*to **be surrounded** [bi sə'raʊndɪd] umgeben sein Unit 4, 48
*to **be willing to** [bi 'wɪlɪŋ tə] wollen, bereit sein Unit 4, 48
*to **become** [bɪ'kʌm] werden Unit 4, 48
bike courier ['baɪk ˌkʊriə] Fahrradkurier Unit 5, 65
to **book** [bʊk] buchen Unit 6, 74
brewery ['brʊəri] Brauerei Unit 4, 46
broken ['brəʊkn] kaputt Unit 1, 11
business course ['bɪznɪs ˌkɔ:s] Wirtschaftskurs Unit 5, 62

C

call centre ['kɔ:l ˌsentə] Call-Center Unit 4, 48
call centre operator [ˌkɔ:l sentər‿'ɒpreɪtə] Call-Center-Mitarbeiter/-in Unit 6, 79
camping site ['kæmpɪŋ ˌsaɪt] Campingplatz Unit 1, 6
Can you tell me the way to ...? [kən ju ˌtel mi ðə 'weɪ tə] Können Sie mir den Weg nach/zu ... sagen? Unit 1, 9
car mechanic [ˌkɑ: mɪ'kænɪk] Kfz-Mechaniker/-in Unit 1, 11
car salesroom [ˌkɑ: 'seɪlzru:m] Verkaufsraum für Autos Unit 3, 39
caretaker ['keəˌteɪkə] Betreuer/-in Unit 4, 51
caring ['keərɪŋ] liebevoll Unit 4, 48
cash [kæʃ] Bargeld Unit 1, 9
cash machine ['kæʃ məˌʃi:n] Bankautomat Unit 1, 9
caterer ['keɪtrə] Speiselieferant/in Unit 1, 11
to **chat** [tʃæt] plaudern Unit 1, 11
city centre [ˌsɪti 'sentə] Stadtmitte Unit 3, 37
cleaner ['kli:nə] Putzkraft Unit 1, 7
clearly ['klɪəli] offensichtlich Unit 6, 73
colleague ['kɒli:g] Kollege/-in Unit 6, 82
comfortable ['kʌmftəbl] bequem, komfortabel Unit 2, 20
company ['kʌmpəni] Gesellschaft, Firma Unit 2, 19 Unit 5, 61
company website [ˌkʌmpəni 'websaɪt] Firmenwebseite Unit 5, 64
complaint [kəm'pleɪnt] Beschwerde Unit 6, 75
confirmation [ˌkɒnfə'meɪʃn] Buchungsbestätigung Unit 6, 74
connection [kə'nekʃn] Verbindung Unit 2, 21
contract ['kɒntrækt] Vertrag Unit 5, 60
couchsurfing ['kaʊtʃˌsɜ:fɪŋ] Couchsurfen Unit 3, 33
creative [kri'eɪtɪv] kreativ Unit 4, 48
customer ['kʌstəmə] Kunde/Kundin Unit 1, 11
customer service agent [ˌkʌstəmə 'sɜ:vɪs 'eɪdʒnt] Kundenbetreuer/-in Unit 4, 48
cute [kju:t] niedlich, süß Unit 4, 50
CV [ˌsi:'vi:] Lebenslauf Unit 5, 60

D

dead [ded] leer, tot Unit 1, 9
*to **deal with** ['di:l wɪð] umgehen mit Unit 5, 62
destination [ˌdestɪ'neɪʃn] Reiseziel Unit 3, 36
different ['dɪfrnt] anders Unit 6, 73
dishwasher ['dɪʃˌwɒʃə] Spülmaschine Unit 2, 20
*to **do a business course** [du‿ə 'bɪznɪs ˌkɔ:s] einen Wirtschaftskurs belegen Unit 6, 76
Don't worry! [ˌdəʊnt 'wʌri] Mach dir keine Sorgen! Unit 6, 73
dos and don'ts [ˌdu:z‿ən 'dəʊnts] was man tun und was man nicht tun sollte Unit 5, 64
double room [ˌdʌbl 'ru:m] Doppelzimmer Unit 6, 74
to **dress** [dres] sich anziehen Unit 6, 73
dressed [drest] angezogen Unit 6, 72
driving licence ['draɪvɪŋ ˌlaɪsns] Führerschein Unit 5, 63
drums [drʌmz] Schlagzeug Unit 1, 15

E

to **earn** [ɜ:n] verdienen Unit 5, 65
education [ˌedʒʊ'keɪʃn] Ausbildung Unit 5, 63
efficiently [ɪ'fɪʃntli] effizient Unit 5, 62
electrician [ˌelɪk'trɪʃn] Elektriker/-in Unit 1, 11
electricity [ˌelɪk'trɪsəti] Strom Unit 2, 20
employment office [ɪm'plɔɪmənt 'ɒfɪs] Agentur für Arbeit Unit 5, 60
energetic [ˌenə'dʒetɪk] voller Energie, energiegeladen Unit 3, 40
engine ['endʒɪn] Motor Unit 1, 11
to **enjoy** [ɪn'dʒɔɪ] gern tun, genießen Unit 5, 65
event organization [ɪ'vent ˌɔ:gnaɪˌzeɪʃn] Veranstaltungsorganisation Unit 5, 62
Excuse me! [ɪk'skju:z mi] Entschuldigung! Unit 1, 9
exhibition hall [ˌeksɪ'bɪʃn ˌhɔ:l] Messehalle Unit 5, 61
experience [ɪk'spɪəriəns] Erfahrung Unit 3, 33
to **explore** [ɪk'splɔ:] erkunden Unit 3, 44

F

factory ['fæktri] Fabrik Unit 4, 46
far [fɑ:] weit Unit 2, 20
farmwork ['fɑ:mwɜ:k] Farmarbeit Unit 3, 32
festival ['festɪvl] Festival, Fest Unit 1, 6
fit [fɪt] gesund, fit Unit 4, 49
flat [flæt] Wohnung Unit 2, 18
flatmate ['flætmeɪt] Mitbewohner/-in Unit 2, 20
flexible ['fleksəbl] flexibel Unit 4, 55
flexible working hours [ˌfleksəbl 'wɜ:kɪŋ‿ˌaʊəz] flexible Arbeitszeit Unit 5, 65
flight [flaɪt] Flug Unit 3, 34
floor [flɔ:] Etage Unit 6, 74
fluent ['flu:ənt] fließend Unit 5, 63
food truck ['fu:d ˌtrʌk] Imbisswagen Unit 1, 6

* = unregelmäßiges Verb; sb. = somebody

foreign country [ˌfɒrən 'kʌntri] Ausland Unit 3, 33
free climbing ['fri: ˌklaɪmɪŋ] Freiklettern Unit 1, 10
furnished ['fɜ:nɪʃt] möbliert Unit 2, 20
furniture ['fɜ:nɪtʃə] Möbel Unit 2, 21

G

grandparents ['grænpeərnts] Großeltern Unit 3, 39
guest [gest] Gast Unit 2, 20
gym [dʒɪm] Fitnesscenter Unit 2, 24

H

hair salon ['heə ˌsælɒn] Friseursalon Unit 2, 22
hairdresser ['heəˌdresə] Friseur/-in Unit 1, 11
hamburger ['hæmˌbɜ:gə] Hamburger Unit 1, 6
*to **hang out with friends** [hæŋ‿'aʊt wɪð 'frendz] sich mit Freunden herumtreiben, abhängen Unit 1, 10
hard-working [ˌhɑ:d'wɜ:kɪŋ] schwer arbeitend Unit 4, 56
heating ['hi:tɪŋ] Heizung Unit 2, 20
helpful ['helpfl] hilfsbereit Unit 4, 48
to **hoover** ['hu:və] staubsaugen Unit 2, 28
host family ['həʊst ˌfæmli] Gastfamilie Unit 3, 34
hostel ['hɒstl] (Jugend-)Herberge Unit 3, 32
housework ['haʊswɜ:k] Hausarbeit Unit 2, 23
*to **hurt** [hɜ:t] verletzen, weh tun Unit 1, 9
husband ['hʌzbənd] Ehemann Unit 3, 44

I

I don't mind [aɪ ˌdəʊnt 'maɪnd] Es ist mir egal Unit 5, 65
I look forward to hearing from you [aɪ lʊk ˌfɔ:wəd tə 'hɪərɪŋ frəm ju:] Ich freue mich von Ihnen zu hören Unit 5, 62
immediately [ɪ'mi:diətli] sofort, gleich Unit 2, 20
impression [ɪm'preʃn] Eindruck Unit 5, 64
in front of [ɪn 'frʌnt‿əv] vor, davor Unit 1, 9
intern ['ɪntɜ:n] Praktikant/-in Unit 2, 19
interview ['ɪntəvju:] Vorstellungsgespräch Unit 5, 60
to **interview** ['ɪntəvju:] befragen Unit 6, 76

J

job advert ['dʒɒb‿ædvɜ:t] Stellenanzeige Unit 3, 40
job application ['dʒɒb‿æplɪˌkeɪʃn] Bewerbung Unit 5, 60
job website [dʒɒb‿wɛbsʌɪt] Online-Jobbörse, Stellenmarkt Unit 5, 60
journey ['dʒɜ:ni] Anfahrt, Fahrt Unit 6, 78

K

kangaroo [ˌkæŋgr'u:] Känguru Unit 3, 32
kindergarten ['kɪndəgɑ:tn] Kindergarten Unit 4, 46

L

to **last** [lɑ:st] anhalten, dauern, bleiben Unit 1, 7
letter of application [ˌletər‿əv‿æplɪ'keɪʃn] Bewerbungsschreiben Unit 5, 64
lively ['laɪvli] belebt, etwas los sein Unit 2, 19
to **look after** [lʊk‿'ɑ:ftə] sich kümmern um Unit 2, 22
to **look forward to** [lʊk ˌfɔ:wəd tə] sich auf etwas freuen Unit 3, 36
lovely ['lʌvli] schön, herrlich Unit 2, 24

M

main [meɪn] Haupt- Unit 1, 11
*to **make a complaint** [ˌmeɪk‿ə kəm'pleɪnt] sich beschweren, reklamieren Unit 6, 73
*to **make appointments** [ˌmeɪk‿ə'pɔɪntmənts] Termine vereinbaren Unit 4, 47
*to **make notes** [ˌmeɪk 'nəʊts] sich Notizen machen Unit 5, 64
maybe ['meɪbi] vielleicht Unit 6, 73
meeting ['mi:tɪŋ] Treffen Unit 5, 61
meeting room ['mi:tɪŋ ˌru:m] Besprechungsraum Unit 6, 73
menu ['menju:] Speisekarte Unit 1, 6
motivated ['məʊtɪveɪtɪd] motiviert Unit 4, 57
motorbike ['məʊtəbaɪk] Motorrad Unit 2, 21
to **move in** [ˌmu:v‿'ɪn] einziehen Unit 2, 21
to **move out** [ˌmu:v‿'aʊt] ausziehen Unit 2, 18
mud [mʌd] Schlamm Unit 1, 6

N

next to ['nekst tə] neben Unit 1, 9

O

Oh dear! [ˌəʊ 'dɪə] Oje! Unit 6, 73
on time [ɒn 'taɪm] pünktlich Unit 3, 42
on your own [ˌɒn jər‿'əʊn] alleine Unit 2, 18
open-minded [ˌəʊpn'maɪndɪd] aufgeschlossen Unit 3, 34
organic farm [ɔ:ˌgænɪk 'fɑ:m] Biohof Unit 4, 57
organized ['ɔ:gnaɪzd] organisiert Unit 4, 48
orientation day [ˌɔ:rien'teɪʃn ˌdeɪ] Orientierungstag Unit 2, 19
outdoors [ˌaʊt'dɔ:z] draußen Unit 4, 49
outfit ['aʊtfɪt] Kleidung Unit 5, 64
outgoing [ˌaʊt'gəʊɪŋ] aufgeschlossen, kontaktfreudig Unit 4, 51

P

package ['pækɪdʒ] Paket Unit 6, 73
paramedic [ˌpærə'medɪk] Sanitäter/-in Unit 1, 9
part [pɑ:t] Teil Unit 1, 11
patient ['peɪʃnt] geduldig Unit 3, 34
*to **pay** [peɪ] zahlen, bezahlen Unit 6, 76
*to **pay attention to detail** [peɪ‿əˌtenʃn tə 'di:teɪl] sorgfältig sein Unit 4, 48
personal assistant ['pɜ:snl‿ə'sɪstnt] persönliche/-r Assistent/-in Unit 1, 11
pet [pet] Haustier Unit 2, 20
placement ['pleɪsmənt] Stelle, Praktikum Unit 4, 46
plane [pleɪn] Flugzeug Unit 3, 32
politely [pə'laɪtli] höflich Unit 5, 62
porter ['pɔ:tə] Gepäckträger Unit 6, 74
to **prepare** [prɪ'peə] vorbereiten Unit 1, 16
properly ['prɒpli] ordentlich Unit 6, 72
*to **put up** [pʊt‿'ʌp] aufstellen Unit 1, 14

Q

qualification [ˌkwɒlɪfɪ'keɪʃn] Qualifikation, Fähigkeit Unit 5, 63

R

raincoat ['reɪnkəʊt] Regenjacke Unit 1, 8
receptionist [rɪ'sepʃnɪst] Empfangsmitarbeiter/-in Unit 6, 74
recharge tent ['ri:tʃɑ:dʒ ˌtent] Zelt, in dem Handys aufgeladen werden können Unit 1, 9
reliable [rɪ'laɪəbl] zuverlässig, vertrauenswürdig Unit 3, 40
removals company [rɪ'mu:vlz ˌkʌmpəni] Umzugsunternehmen Unit 2, 26
removals man [rɪ'mu:vlz ˌmæn] Umzugshelfer Unit 2, 26
rent [rent] Miete Unit 2, 20
to **repeat** [rɪ'pi:t] wiederholen Unit 3, 37

requirement [rɪ'kwaɪəmənt] Anforderung Unit 4, 56
routine [ru:'ti:n] Routine, Tagesablauf Unit 2, 22
rubbish ['rʌbɪʃ] Müll Unit 2, 23
rude [ru:d] unhöflich Unit 4, 48

S

salary ['sælri] Lohn, Gehalt Unit 3, 34
sales assistant ['seɪlz‿ə,sɪstnt] Verkaufsangestellte/-r Unit 1, 15
sensitive ['sensətɪv] sensibel, einfühlsam Unit 4, 50
separate ['seprət] separat, getrennt Unit 2, 20
to **serve** [sɜ:v] ausschenken, servieren Unit 1, 16
to **share** [ʃeə] teilen Unit 2, 18
shared flat [ʃeəd 'flæt] Wohngemeinschaft Unit 2, 18
shift [ʃɪft] Schicht, Dienst Unit 2, 19
shower [ʃaʊə] Dusche Unit 2, 20
sick [sɪk] krank Unit 4, 47
sight [saɪt] Sehenswürdigkeit Unit 3, 32
single room [,sɪŋgl 'ru:m] Einzelzimmer Unit 6, 74
skills [skɪlz] Kenntnisse, Fähigkeiten Unit 5, 61
skyscraper ['skaɪskreɪpə] Hochhaus, Wolkenkratzer Unit 2, 18
soccer ['sɒkə] Fußball Unit 1, 15
spare room [speə 'ru:m] Gästezimmer Unit 3, 38
*to **spend** [spend] verbringen Unit 2, 19
sporty ['spɔ:ti] sportlich Unit 4, 48
stage [steɪdʒ] Bühne Unit 1, 6
still [stɪl] noch, immer noch Unit 2, 19
stressed [strest] gestresst Unit 6, 72
studio flat [stju:diəʊ 'flæt] Apartment, Studio Unit 2, 20
suitable ['su:təbl] passend, geeignet Unit 5, 64
surgery ['sɜ:dʒri] Arztpraxis Unit 4, 46

T

*to **take care of sb.** [teɪk‿'keər‿əv ,sʌmbədi] sich um jemanden kümmern Unit 3, 33
*to **take initiative** [teɪk ɪ'nɪʃətɪv] Initiative ergreifen Unit 3, 40
*to **take orders** [teɪk 'ɔ:dərs] Bestellungen aufnehmen Unit 1, 11
*to **take place** [,teɪk 'pleɪs] stattfinden Unit 1, 8
to **taste** [teɪst] schmecken Unit 2, 24
tent [tent] Zelt Unit 1, 6
ticket office clerk [,tɪkɪt‿ɒfɪs 'klɑ:k] Mitarbeiter/-in am Fahrkartenschalter Unit 6, 78
to **tidy** ['taɪdi] aufräumen Unit 2, 23
tidy ['taɪdi] ordentlich Unit 4, 56
tool [tu:l] Werkzeug Unit 6, 73
tour guide ['tʊə ,gaɪd] Reiseleiter/-in Unit 4, 48
traffic ['træfɪk] Verkehr Unit 6, 74
to **train** [treɪn] eine Ausbildung machen Unit 5, 61
train trip ['treɪn ,trɪp] Zugfahrt Unit 3, 37
trainee electrician [,treɪni:‿,elɪk'trɪʃn] Elektriker/-in in der Ausbildung Unit 2, 22
trainee team assistant [,treɪni: 'ti:m‿ə,sɪstənt] Teamassistent/-in in der Ausbildung Unit 5, 61
training camp ['treɪnɪŋ ,kæmp] Freizeit für Kinder Unit 5, 65
transport company ['trænspɔ:t ,kʌmpəni] Transportfirma Unit 5, 63
to **travel** ['trævl] reisen Unit 3, 32
to **travel on your own** [,trævl‿ɒn jər‿'əʊn] alleine reisen Unit 3, 38
to **travel with a friend** [,trævl wɪð‿ə 'frend] mit einem Freund/einer Freundin zusammen reisen Unit 3, 38
traveller ['trævlə] Reisende/-r Unit 3, 37
to **turn** [tɜ:n] abbiegen, wenden Unit 1, 9
to **turn off** [,tɜ:n‿'ɒf] ausschalten Unit 5, 64

U

unfriendly [ʌn'frendli] unfreundlich Unit 6, 75
unhappy [ʌn'hæpi] unglücklich Unit 6, 77
useful ['ju:sfl] nützlich Unit 6, 81

V

veterinary assistant ['vetrɪnri‿ə,sɪstənt] Tierarzthelfer/-in Unit 4, 49
view [vju:] Ausblick Unit 6, 74
village ['vɪlɪdʒ] Dorf Unit 2, 18
vocational college [və,keɪʃnl 'kɒlɪdz] Berufskolleg Unit 5, 62

W

waiter/waitress ['weɪtə, 'weɪtrəs] Kellner/-in, Bedienung Unit 1, 11
to **walk straight on** [wɔ:k ,streɪt‿'ɒn] geradeaus gehen Unit 1, 9
wardrobe ['wɔ:drəʊb] Kleiderschrank Unit 2, 20
to **wash up** [wɒʃ‿'ʌp] abwaschen, Geschirr spülen Unit 2, 22
washing machine ['wɒʃɪŋ məʃi:n] Waschmaschine Unit 2, 20
wellingtons ['welɪŋtnz] Gummistiefel Unit 1, 6
wife [waɪf] Ehefrau Unit 3, 37
wine [waɪn] Wein Unit 5, 62
to **wish** [wɪʃ] wünschen, wollen Unit 5, 62
work experience [,wɜ:k‿ɪk'spɪəriəns] Berufserfahrung Unit 5, 61
work placement ['wɜ:k ,pleɪsmənt] Berufspraktikum Unit 5, 63
to **work** [wɜ:k] funktionieren Unit 6, 73
working hours [,wɜ:kɪŋ‿'aʊəz] Arbeitszeit Unit 3, 34
wristband ['rɪstbænd] Eintrittsbändchen Unit 1, 6

Numbers, dates and times

Cardinal numbers			
1	one	17	seventeen
2	two	18	eighteen
3	three	19	nineteen
4	four	20	twenty
5	five	21	twenty-one
6	six	22	twenty-two
7	seven	30	thirty
8	eight	31	thirty-one
9	nine	40	forty
10	ten	50	fifty
11	eleven	60	sixty
12	twelve	70	seventy
13	thirteen	80	eighty
14	fourteen	90	ninety
15	fifteen	100	a hundred
16	sixteen	110	a hundred and ten

Ordinal numbers			
1st	first	17th	seventeenth
2nd	second	18th	eighteenth
3rd	third	19th	nineteenth
4th	fourth	20th	twentieth
5th	fifth	21st	twenty-first
6th	sixth	22nd	twenty-second
7th	seventh	30th	thirtieth
8th	eighth	31st	thirty-first
9th	ninth	40th	fortieth
10th	tenth	50th	fiftieth
11th	eleventh	60th	sixtieth
12th	twelfth	70th	seventieth
13th	thirteenth	80th	eightieth
14th	fourteenth	90th	ninetieth
15th	fifteenth	100th	hundredth
16th	sixteenth		

1,000 a thousand • 1,000,000 (1m) a million • 1,000,000,000 (1bn) a billion
1.5 one point five • 2.73 two point seven three • 27% twenty-seven per cent
½ a half • ¼ a quarter • ¾ three quarters • ⅓ a third • ⅕ a fifth
£1.50 one pound fifty • 99p ninety-nine p/pence • $12.20 twelve dollars twenty

Dates	
Write …	**Say …**
1 October	the first of October
2 January	the second of January
3 August	the third of August
4 November	the fourth of November
20 April	the twentieth of April
25 May	the twenty-fifth of May
30 March	the thirtieth of March

Years	
1900	nineteen hundred
1901	nineteen oh one
1985	nineteen eighty-five
2000	two thousand
2001	two thousand and one
2005	two thousand and five
2010	twenty-ten
2015	twenty-fifteen

The 12-hour clock			
	twelve o'clock midday/midnight		twenty-five past ten
	five past ten		half past ten
	ten past ten		twenty-five to eleven
	(a) quarter past ten		(a) quarter to eleven
	twenty past ten		five to eleven

The 24-hour clock			
12:00	twelve o'clock midday	13:00	one o'clock in the afternoon / thirteen hundred
00:00	twelve o'clock midnight		
10:05	ten oh five	13:07	thirteen oh seven
10:10	ten ten	15:30	fifteen thirty
10:15	ten fifteen	18:56	eighteen fifty-six

Classroom phrases

Asking about words and meanings	
What does (the word) … mean?	Was bedeutet (das Wort) …?
I don't understand the word …/ the expression …/this sentence.	Ich verstehe das Wort … nicht/ den Ausdruck … nicht/diesen Satz nicht.
How do you say … in English?	Wie sagt man … auf Englisch?
Could you repeat that/say that again?	Könnten Sie das wiederholen/nochmal sagen?
Giving your opinion	
I think (that) …	Ich denke/meine, dass …
In my opinion …	Meiner Meinung nach …
I find … (really) good/interesting/boring.	Ich finde … (echt) gut/interessant/langweilig.
Agreeing and disagreeing	
I agree (with Martina).	Ich stimme (Martina) zu.
I disagree/don't agree (with Bernd).	Ich stimme (Bernd) nicht zu.
Yes, I think the same/I think that, too.	Ja, ich denke das Gleiche/das meine ich auch.
Rubbish!	Quatsch!
Talking about texts	
In the text the reader learns that …	Im Text erfährt der Leser/die Leserin, dass …
The first paragraph tells us that …	Der erste Absatz sagt uns, dass …
In the second paragraph we read/learn that …	Im zweiten Absatz liest/erfährt man, dass …
The last paragraph is about …	Im letzten Absatz geht es um …
In the text it (also) says that …	Im Text steht (auch), dass …
Finally, we learn/read that …	Zuletzt lernt/liest man, dass …
Working in class	
Would you write that on the board, please?	Würden Sie das bitte an die Tafel schreiben?
Could you play the CD again, please?	Würden Sie die CD bitte nochmal vorspielen?
I'm not sure what we have to do.	Ich bin nicht sicher, was wir tun müssen.
I haven't got a partner.	Ich habe keinen Partner/keine Partnerin.
We need another person in our group.	Unserer Gruppe fehlt eine Person.
Our group is ready/has finished.	Unsere Gruppe ist fertig.
We need a bit more time.	Wir brauchen noch ein bisschen Zeit.
Could I borrow a/your dictionary?	Darf ich ein/Ihr Wörterbuch ausleihen?

complete	ergänzen Sie
find (out)	finden Sie (heraus)
missing	fehlend
match	ordnen Sie zu
choose	wählen Sie
translate	übersetzen Sie
put in the correct order	stellen Sie in die richtige Reihenfolge
make notes/note down	notieren Sie
make a summary	fassen Sie zusammen
correct	korrigieren Sie
practise	üben Sie
imagine	stellen Sie sich vor
invent … yourself	erfinden Sie (selbst)
talk about/discuss	diskutieren Sie
do a survey	machen Sie eine Umfrage
give a talk	halten Sie eine Rede
which mean the same/have the same meaning	die die gleiche Bedeutung haben
which mean the opposite/have the opposite meaning	die die entgegengesetzte Bedeutung haben
in your own words	in eigenen Worten

Countries in which English is the / an official language

NAME Independent Commonwealth sta

Name Dependent territories of Commonwealth states (in brackets) SCALE 1 : 88,000,000

ORKNEY ISLANDS
OUTER HEBRIDES
Inverness
Aberdeen
Loch Ness
Ben Nevis
SCOTLAND
Glasgow
Edinburgh
Hadrian's Wall
Tyne
Newcastle
NORTHERN IRELAND
Belfast
ISLE OF MAN
Lake District
York
Hull
Irish Sea
Galway
Dublin
REPUBLIC OF IRELAND
Liverpool
Manchester
Snowdon
Nottingham
Trent
ENGLAND
Birmingham
Severn
Cambridge
North Se
Cork
WALES
Big Ben
Oxford
London
Thames
Margate
Cardiff
Dover
Stonehenge
Brighton
Devon
ISLE OF WIGHT
Cornwall
Plymouth
ISLES OF SCILLY
English Channel

Video-Tutorials

Unit 1

V 1 **1** TUTORIAL **Getting to know people**

A 3 **d)** **Andrew:** Hi everyone, this is Andrew from *Channel Cool!* Today we want to show you how to get to know people. Benjamin, Rebecca and Emily are having breakfast at the moment. I'll go over and introduce myself. Let's see what happens!
Good morning guys. Can I sit with you?
Rebecca: Oh sure, sit down. Good morning!
Andrew: Are you a group of friends?
Emily: Yes, we are, but we're from all over the world. I'm Emily, I live in London. What's your name?
Andrew: My name's Andrew. Nice to meet you, Emily.
Benjamin: I'm Benjamin. I come from Brisbane in Australia.
Andrew: Wow, Australia! That's a long way from here!
Rebecca: I'm from Manchester, my name is Rebecca. Where are you from?
Andrew: I was born in London but now I live in Dallas. That's in the United States of America.
Benjamin: Wow, an international breakfast. I like it!
Andrew: Now you know how to get to know people. And you can tell them who you are. Thanks for joining us here on *Channel Cool!*

V 2 **2** TUTORIAL **Talking about yourself**

A4 **Rebecca:** Welcome to *Channel Cool!* So, you've just met some new people and you want to find out more about them? We'll show you how it's done! Andrew seems to be really nice – let's find out more about him! So, Andrew, are you here on holidays?
Andrew: Yes, I'm travelling through Europe and I'm here to see my favorite band tonight.
Benjamin: Wow, that sounds like a great plan! What kind of music do you like?
Andrew: Heavy metal!
Rebecca: Oh no, really?
Emily: I agree with Rebecca. I also don't like heavy metal. But I like listening to hard rock.
Andrew: Nobody here likes heavy metal? Come on, Benjamin, help me out.
Benjamin: Sorry, I don't really like music. I'm more into sport. Free climbing is amazing.
Andrew: Really? Wow, that's exciting. But you can only go climbing in summer, right?
Benjamin: No, you can go climbing in winter too. There are climbing walls indoors.
Rebecca: Sounds interesting guys, but climbing is too stressful for me. Shopping or … hanging out with my friends – those are my hobbies.
Emily: I agree. We should look for a nice shopping mall today, Rebecca!
Rebecca: That sounds great!
See, that was easy! Now you know what you can ask other people and how to talk about yourself! Thank you for joining us on *Channel Cool!*

V 3 **3** TUTORIAL **Talking about jobs**

A 5 **Emily:** Hi again, this is Emily for *Channel Cool!* Today I want to tell you something about different jobs. Let's start with a job that is very popular – and not only with boys: Lots of people want to be a car mechanic. If you like working with cars and don't have a problem when your hands get dirty and greasy, this is the perfect job for you! You change tyres, repair engines and replace broken parts. You also check the electronic systems in a car. You can work in a small garage that only deals with one brand or a big garage where you can work on cars of all kinds and sizes.
Do you like working with people? Are you into beauty? Well, you could think about a job as a hairdresser. Your main tasks are cutting, colouring and blow-drying hair. And you also chat to your customers, of course. But I think a hairdresser does so much more: you can help customers to find a new look and style and who knows, you could even change their lives!
Now, let me tell you about a job that never goes out of fashion: working in a shop. A sales assistant puts products onto shelves and helps customers to find what they need. Of course a sales assistant also tidies up after customers. Just think of all the places a shop assistant can work: in shops that sell sports equipment or electronic equipment or clothes. You can even turn your hobby into a career – for example, if you like computer games, you can work in a store that sells them.
Working as an electrician is perfect if you want a technical job. An electrician does many different things. You can go to people's homes to repair the lighting system, or lay cables on a building site, or install security cameras in a factory or check the electrical equipment in an office. Every day is different!
If you like meeting lots of people you can work as a waiter or waitress. Your main tasks are taking orders, setting and clearing tables. Of course, you also bring people food and drinks. There are many options: you could work in a small café, a lively pub or a posh restaurant! The job never gets boring but let me be honest: you always have to be friendly, even when customers are not polite or you're not in a good mood!
As you can see, there are a lot of great jobs out there. I hope one of them is interesting for you. Thank you for listening to *Channel Cool!*

Unit 2

1 TUTORIAL Talking about routines

V 4
A 12

Rebecca: Hi, this is Rebecca for *Channel Cool!* Today we want to show you what happens when you look at a room in a shared flat: what can you say about yourself? What questions will people ask you? Hey guys, let's do a little role play! Andrew and I live in a shared flat and Benjamin comes to look at a room!
Andrew: Great idea, Rebecca!
Rebecca: Hi Benjamin. Great to meet you.
Benjamin: Hi Rebecca. Hi Andrew.
Andrew: Hi.
Rebecca: Do you come from around here? Do you know the area a bit?
Benjamin: Oh no, I come from Brisbane actually.
Rebecca: Brisbane, Australia? That's amazing! My sister also lives in Australia. She works for an international company. I come from Manchester and Andrew comes from London. But he usually lives in Dallas in the United States. What do you do?
Benjamin: I work for a removals company. I'm a trainee mechanic so I have to look after the lorries.
Andrew: That sounds like hard work. I'm a trainee electrician. Do you work at the weekend, Benjamin?
Benjamin: Yes, I often work on Saturdays.
Rebecca: Me, too. I work in a hair salon and I always work on Saturday. What time do you – do you start work?
Benjamin: I usually start at 7 in the morning. That means I have to get up at 6.
Rebecca: That's perfect. We never get up before 7 so you can go into the bathroom before us.
Benjamin: That sounds great! I work a night shift sometimes. That means I have to work at night and sleep during the day.
Andrew: That's no problem. Rebecca and I never come home before 6:30. So the flat is quiet and you can sleep during the day.
Rebecca: Oh, and we always cook together on Thursdays. Is that ok?
Benjamin: That sounds great! I don't cook but I can wash up!
Andrew: Perfect. Benjamin wants to wash up. Now we don't have to buy a dishwasher! Thanks for joining us here on *Channel Cool!* Now you know how to talk about yourself and answer people's questions.

2 TUTORIAL Talking about housework and money

V 5
A 13

Rebecca: This is *Channel Cool!* again. Today we want to show you how you can talk about two difficult topics in a shared flat: housework and money. Let's do a little role play! Andrew and I live in a shared flat and Ben is interested in a room.
Andrew: Let's see how that goes.
Rebecca: Ok, Benjamin. So we all do different jobs in the flat. If you want to move in, you also have to help out.
Benjamin: Do you want me to help with the housework?
Andrew: Yes, of course. Tomorrow is Monday, right? So I take out the rubbish and I also clean the kitchen on Monday.
Rebecca: Then on Wednesday I have to clean the bathroom. I do that after work because then the bathroom is free.
Benjamin: I see. What other things do you do?
Rebecca: Well, on Friday someone has to hoover the living room. But before you hoover the living room, you have to tidy it.
Benjamin: Okay, sounds good. Hoover and tidy up – I can do that!
Rebecca: Then the next week we all do a different job. Your room is private and you are responsible for keeping it clean.
Andrew: The other thing we want to talk about is money.
Benjamin: Ok. How much does the room cost?
Rebecca: The room costs £250 a month.
Benjamin: £250, I see … And how much do you pay for heating?
Rebecca: We pay £50 a month for heating, electricity and Wi-Fi. Oh, and we all pay £20 a month for the food that we need for our cooking nights.
Benjamin: I see. That's expensive. I only get £650 a month. But it is a really nice room …
Andrew: And you would be a nice flatmate. So now you know how to talk about difficult things like housework and money. Thanks for joining us here on *Channel Cool!*

Unit 3

1 TUTORIAL Finding a place to stay

V 6
A21

Emily: Hello and welcome to *Channel Cool!* Today we want to talk about going on holidays when you don't have much money.
Andrew: That's right. The biggest problem is finding a cheap place to stay. Let's do a role play, Emily!
Emily: Great idea, Andrew! Let's go. … Hey!
Andrew: Hey, Emily. I really need a holiday. I think I'll go away for a long weekend.
Emily: Oh, where do you want to go?
Andrew: Well, I met some people from Dublin last year and there are a lot of things to do there.
Emily: Sounds like a good idea. And when do you want to go?
Andrew: I asked my boss and I can take one or two days off in April. I think from 10 to 13 April.
Emily: So that's four days altogether. Three nights in a hotel is expensive, you know?

Andrew: Yes, I need a cheap place to stay because I have to pay for the flight. And I want to have some money to do things, too.
Emily: Of course. You know there are websites where people offer a bed or a sofa to travellers.
Andrew: You're right. I spent a night on someone's sofa when I went to Berlin last year. It was really great.
Emily: Berlin! Sounds great. Are you travelling with someone?
Andrew: No, I'm travelling on my own but I think Dublin's a great city to meet new people.
Emily: Yeah, of course. What kind of host are you looking for?
Andrew: I'm looking for a friendly host who lives near the city centre. I don't want to take the bus. I hope my host can tell me about interesting events and sights around Dublin. I want to see a lot of things in the four days.
Emily: Well, you can start by looking online.
Andrew: That's the first step to my holiday. Now you know where you can find a cheap place to stay. Thanks for joining me and Emily on *Channel Cool!*

3 TUTORIAL Meeting your host

V 7
A 23

Andrew: Hi, here are Andrew …
Emily: … and Emily
Andrew: … from *Channel Cool!* again. Do you remember? Last time I called my host Mary in Dublin, now it's time to meet her! We'll do a little role play again. Emily, you can be Mary.
Emily: Ok Andrew, I'm Mary.
Andrew: We'll show you how to get to know your host and talk about you and your family.
Hi. I'm Andrew. Are you Mary?
Emily: Yes, that's right. Welcome to Dublin, Andrew. Please come in.
Andrew: Thanks.
Emily: Oh, would you like a cup of tea?
Andrew: Yes, please!
Emily: So, how was your trip?
Andrew: Fine thanks. The plane was on time and the bus driver was very helpful. He told me funny stories about his holidays in the US.
Emily: Oh, I believe you. Do you have a big family in the US?
Andrew: Yes, I do. My family lives in Dallas. I've a younger brother and sister.
Emily: Do they work?
Andrew: No, they're still at school. They're 13 and 16 years old.
Emily: OK. And what do your parents do?
Andrew: They have a car salesroom in Dallas. When things get busy, my grandparents and my uncle help out too. So it's a real family business. My sister is always there after school. I think she'll be a great saleswoman one day.
Emily: You can never start too early! Would you like another cup of tea before my daughter comes home? She's still at my mother's house.
Andrew: That sounds great. Thank you.
Emily: Oh, and help yourself! I hope you enjoyed our little role play! Now you know what to say to your host! And you can make small talk and talk about your family. Please join us again soon on *Channel Cool!*

Unit 4

1 TUTORIAL Looking at job adverts

V 8
A 30

Rebecca: Welcome back to *Channel Cool!* This is Rebecca and we have an interesting topic today: job adverts and finding out what jobs are suitable for you – or not. I think Andrew has already started looking at adverts. I'll go and talk to him. Hey Andrew, you're home already. What are you doing?
Andrew: Hey, Rebecca. I'm looking at some really cool advertisements for summer jobs. I don't have much money at the moment so maybe this is a nice way to see another country.
Rebecca: Great idea! Show me what you've found.
Andrew: This is my favourite advert: wombat babysitter in Australia! I've always wanted to go to Australia and look at that cute little wombat!
Rebecca: He is very cute but you know how expensive flights to Australia are!
Andrew: They will pay for the flight.
Rebecca: Okay then. But what kind of job experience is wombat babysitting? You won't work in a zoo later!
Andrew: But I would still have a great time in Australia!
Rebecca: Yes, if you take somebody with you to the island, and who will that be? No, not me! I'm allergic to animal hair. And look, it says that there are no people on the island. Won't the job be too boring for you?
Andrew: You're right, maybe Australia's not such a good idea.
Rebecca: There must be other jobs. Let's take another look!
Andrew: Okay, I'm not going to Australia. But I still need a summer job. Now you know what things to look for in an advert. Thanks for joining us here on *Channel Cool!*

2 TUTORIAL Finding the right summer job

V 9
A 32

Andrew: Hi, this is Andrew from *Channel Cool!* I'm still trying to find a summer job that suits me and Rebecca is still trying to help me. I think she's found something. Let's find out what it is.
Rebecca: Look at this advert, Andrew. They want an island caretaker in Sweden.
Andrew: That sounds good! Not as warm as Australia though!

Rebecca: Let's see what they want. You must be friendly and good with people.
Andrew: Well yes, I think I am. I worked as a waiter during school holidays and my boss was very happy with my work.
Rebecca: And the job in Sweden will be outdoors. That's perfect for you!
Andrew: That's true. The job sounds like the project we did after school last year! We had to keep the local parks and playgrounds clean.
Rebecca: Oh, I didn't know that. That sounds so nice!
Andrew: And look, I would also have the chance to become a team leader. That will look good on my CV later!
Rebecca: Looks like they won't pay you any money but you won't have to pay for your room or food.
Andrew: Sounds like a good deal. And the flight won't be as expensive as a flight to Australia.
I think I can afford it.
Rebecca: They want to see your CV. Do you have one already?
Andrew: No. But I have some ideas. I will read the advert more closely and make a list next weekend.
Rebecca: Now you know what things to look for in an advert: the job must suit your interests. And you should learn something new. The question is: is the job good enough to put on your CV? Thank you for being with us today. We're Rebecca and Andrew for *Channel Cool!*

Unit 5

1 TUTORIAL Dos and don'ts at a job interview

V 10
A 40

Benjamin: Hi, this is Benjamin from *Channel Cool!*
Today I want to tell you how to prepare for a job interview.
First of all: the day before you go to your interview, it's important that you look at the job advert once again carefully. You can also check the company website again.
Make sure you check your letter of application once again. Which qualifications did you mention? How did you introduce yourself?
You can also make notes and bring your notebook with you to the interview: write down what you want to say about yourself and what questions YOU want to ask about the job.
Now that you're prepared, you have to think about your outfit. It's very important to make a good first impression!
This is Rebecca. She's going to an interview but not dressed like that! Wear suitable clothes, Rebecca – just like Andrew over here. Very nice, Andrew!
But finish your coffee before the interview!
And turn off your phone!
It's very important to be polite and that includes turning off your phone! Be friendly to people: smile and look them in the eye when you're speaking with them.
Emily: Oh no, am I too late for our tutorial?
Benjamin: And be on time!
Now you know how to prepare for a job interview.
And you also know what not to do in an interview!
The four of us wish you good luck! See you soon on *Channel Cool!*

2 TUTORIAL Doing a good job interview

V 11
A 41

Emily: Hi, this is Emily from *Channel Cool!* Now it's time for your job interview. Maybe you're nervous because you don't know what the interviewer will ask you. No problem! Andrew and Rebecca will show you what to say and what you don't say in an interview.
Please tell me something about yourself.
Andrew: I finished school last year and I've worked as a bike courier for six months. I like partying and getting up late.
Rebecca: Well, I'm 18 years old and I'm doing a course at a vocational college. I'll finish this course in June this year. I'd love to work as a trainee in event organization at your company.
Emily: Why do you want to work for us?
Andrew: Because you earn good money and you have flexible working hours. But actually, I've applied for several jobs. I don't mind which company I work for.
Rebecca: Your company has a very good name in event organization. I've been to some of your events: I went to the street food festival in the city park last summer. I thought it was well organized and I really enjoyed it. I feel like I would learn a lot working with you.
Emily: Why should we choose you for the traineeship?
Andrew: Um…
Rebecca: Well, I read in your advert that you're looking for someone who's well organized and who works well in a team. I do a lot for our local youth club. I've helped to organize the summer training camp for the last two years. I really enjoyed working in a team and organizing fun activities for young people.
Emily: Do you have any questions?
Andrew: No. Are we finished?
Rebecca: Yes! I read on your website that the trainees will work in different parts of the company. Can you tell me more about that?
Emily: What do you think – who did a better interview? Thanks for being with us on *Channel Cool!*

Unit 6

V 12 A 49 2 TUTORIAL Dealing with problems with your boss

Benjamin: Today we're talking about difficult situations at work. What do you say when your boss complains about your work? Let's do a role play and look at a typical situation. Rebecca is my boss and I was late for work today.
Rebecca: Why did you come in late today, Benjamin? It's the second time this week!
Benjamin: I'm sorry. My train was late today.
Rebecca: Well, maybe you should think about taking an earlier train so you can be on time! The rest of the team had to wait for you, again.
Benjamin: I know, you're right. But we were only 20 minutes late at the customer's house.
Rebecca: That was the problem! The customer was really angry that he had to wait for you for 20 minutes.
Benjamin: I'm really sorry. It won't happen again.
Rebecca: Okay then, let's go back to work now.
Benjamin: Well, now you know how to say you're sorry when your boss complains. See you again soon on *Channel Cool!*

V 13 A 50 3 TUTORIAL Dealing with a difficult situation

Emily: Hello and welcome to *Channel Cool!* This is Emily. So let's look at a difficult situation with an angry customer – what do you say to them? Andrew and I will do a role play. I work in a hotel and Andrew is a guest. Let's see what happens.
Andrew: Hello, I'm Andrew Young.
Emily: Welcome Mr Young! I hope you had a good journey.
Andrew: It was okay, but I got stuck in traffic twice.
Emily: I'm sorry to hear that. There's always a lot of traffic on Fridays. You've booked a room for two nights …
Andrew: Yes, a room with a king-size bed.
Emily: I'll have a look. Oh I'm sorry, but I only have a room with a single bed.
Andrew: That can't be right. Look, here is the e-mail confirmation from your hotel. And it says: king-size bed!
Emily: Yes, I'm very sorry, that was our mistake. Um, what can we do? Oh, I just see you have booked breakfast. Breakfast normally costs 15 euros per day, but you won't have to pay for it. Would that be okay?
Andrew: Okay, if you really don't have any other room.
Emily: No, I'm afraid we don't. I can give you a quiet room with a nice view of the river.
Andrew: Thanks for the offer. Now you know what to say to a customer in a difficult situation – always be polite and always say you're sorry. We're Andrew and Emily from *Channel Cool!* Thanks for being with us!

Hörtexte

Unit 1

A 1 2 Listening: At the Hurricane festival

Laura: Hi, this is Laura May from *Radio Light*. Today I'm at the *Hurricane festival* in Scheeßel. For people who don't know Scheeßel it's a small town in the north of Germany! Can you imagine? Every year the famous *Hurricane festival* takes place here. The festival is all about rock music. 100 bands play here in three days. That makes a total of 38 hours of music! The tickets cost from 180 to 550 euros for the whole festival. That's a lot of money! Fans with a cheaper ticket are allowed to put up a tent on the camping site with 20,000 other people. People with an expensive ticket can sleep in a resort. No matter which ticket you buy, you can enjoy three days of great music and party with more than 70,000 fans. 5,000 people work at the festival and make sure that everyone has a good time. Maybe the most important helpers are the cleaners of the 1,700 toilets. So, for all fans of live music: the *Hurricane festival* is the place to go!

A 8 2 Test yourself: At a festival

1. Calling the owner of a red sports car with the number HB O 2211. Please come to the information desk. That's the owner of a red sports car with the number HB O2211.
2. Please listen everybody. There's a storm coming from the north in the next hour. We have to stop the festival for the next hour. A storm is coming. Please stay safe!
3. To all hungry people out there, there's a new food truck behind stage number 2. That's behind stage number 2. There you can buy great pulled pork burgers!
4. To all fans who can't get enough music and dancing and partying, you can come to the after-hours party on the grass next to the camping site. The after-hours party starts at midnight. So don't be late. See you next to the camping site at midnight!
5. Please remember that the camping site closes two hours after the last concert. I repeat we close the camping site two hours after the last concert finishes.

Unit 2

A 10 2 Listening: A room for Jannik

Jannik: So Patrick, where do you live in Ireland?
Patrick: I normally live in a flat near Cork City. I want to move in with my girlfriend Sheena when I finish here next month.
Jannik: Wow, that sounds cool. Do you want to move into your girlfriend's flat?
Patrick: No, she shares a flat with two other girls. We're looking for a two-bedroom flat at the moment. How about you?

Jannik: I live at home. It's comfortable and cheap but it's a bit far from Stuttgart.
Patrick: Why don't you move to Stuttgart?
Jannik: I can't afford my own flat.
Patrick: Well, I have a room in a shared flat in Stuttgart. It'll be free from the beginning of April. Are you interested?
Jannik: Yes, I am. How much is the room?
Patrick: The rent is € 300 a month.
Jannik: How much do you pay for heating and electricity?
Patrick: We pay € 50 a month for heating and electricity. So that's € 350 altogether.
Jannik: What are the people in the flat like?
Patrick: Paolo is a student from Italy and Sofia comes from Sweden. We're very international and it's great fun.
Jannik: Uh oh, do you speak English then?
Patrick: Yes, but your English is very good!
Jannik: Well, thanks. Is the room furnished?
Patrick: Yes, it is. There's a bed, a chair, a desk and a wardrobe. You can have them if you like.
Jannik: Really? That sounds great. And is the flat far from work?
Patrick: It's about 15 minutes by bus. The bus stop is in front of the flat.
Jannik: It sounds perfect. Can I have a look at the room?
Patrick: Yes, of course! You can visit us next weekend!

A 14 3 TUTORIAL Asking people what they do

Rebecca: This is Rebecca for *Channel Cool!* Andrew and I asked Benjamin to stay for dinner. We want to know more about him. Listen carefully so you can ask people questions about what they do every day.
Benjamin: That was a really lovely dinner. Thanks a lot! Where did you learn to cook?
Rebecca: Thanks Benjamin! I often helped my grandmother and I learned a lot from her.
Benjamin: Sounds great! Do you often cook?
Rebecca: Yes, I usually cook three times a week when I finish work at 5.
Benjamin: When do you finish work the other days?
Rebecca: Well our salon closes at 8 but sometimes it takes about 30 minutes longer to clean up.
Benjamin: Wow, do you have time for hobbies then?
Rebecca: Well, cooking is my hobby I guess.
Benjamin: What about you, Andrew?
Andrew: I play football twice a week with friends. And I go to the gym sometimes. That's better when I work shifts.
Rebecca: Why?
Andrew: Because the gym opens early and closes really late. How often do you do night shifts, Benjamin?
Benjamin: Not so often. Most of the time I start work at 7 in the morning and finish at 4. But every three weeks I have to work night shifts. They start at 10 p.m. and finish at 6 a.m.
Rebecca: You work when other people sleep. How does that feel, Benjamin?
Benjamin: At the beginning it feels strange, but you get used to it.
Andrew: That was interesting! Now you know how to ask people questions about what they do. Join us again soon on *Channel Cool!*

A 18 Test yourself: Aufgabe e)

Florence: Come in. The door's open.
Johannes: Hello Luke.
Luke: Hi, you two. This is my girlfriend, Sophia.
Sophia: Hi Florence, hi Johannes. Thanks for the invitation.
Johannes: Welcome to our floating home.
Sophia: The flowers are for you, Florence.
Florence: What nice flowers! Thank you!
Luke: Well, Sophia is a trainee in a flower shop.
Florence: Are you? That's a lovely job. I love flowers.
Sophia: Me too. The shop is near here. You can normally find me there 6 days a week and I often don't get home before 7 o'clock.
Luke: That's why I always cook in the evenings. Sophia doesn't want to cook when she gets home late.
Florence: What do you do, Luke?
Luke: I'm a carpenter and I make furniture in a workshop. What about you, Johannes? Where do you come from in Germany?
Johannes: I come from Hamburg. We have a lot of water in Hamburg and that's why I love living on a houseboat.
Sophia: Here's to houseboats. Cheers.
Florence, Luke, Johannes: Cheers.

Unit 3

A 19 2 Listening: Cheap travel options

You want to see the world but you don't have much money? Then maybe working in a foreign country is perfect for you! Let's listen to three people who spent some time working abroad.
Lisa: Hey, my name is Lisa. I'm 19 years old and I spent a year in Canada last year. I had a great time! I lived with a host family and worked as an au pair. That means that I took care of the two children: I made breakfast for them in the morning, I brought them to school and kindergarten – and of course I also played a lot with them. But at the weekends I always had time to explore the country and to visit interesting sights. If you want to work as an au pair, you need to be at least 18 years old. You also need to have some experience

working with children, for example as a babysitter or as a helper in a youth club. And you need to be patient when the children are lively!

Jake: Hi, I'm Jake. I came back home after a year in Australia last week. I travelled around the country and worked on farms to earn money for my travels. The good thing was: I was also allowed to live on the farms. So I didn't need money for a hostel. I did many different tasks on the farms: for example I helped to milk the cows, I picked apples on a fruit farm, and I learned how to change tyres on a tractor. So if you like working outside and if you're fit, farmwork might be fun for you! And on your days off you can visit cities or just relax on the farm.

Hannah: Hey, this is Hannah from Ireland! I wanted to spend some time travelling through England and Scotland last summer. I didn't have much money – so I went on a website to find people who let travellers sleep on their couch. I had so much fun getting to know my hosts and many of them showed me the sights in their cities. If you want to try couchsurfing, you need to be friendly and open-minded. And of course you have to like meeting new people.

A 22 2 TUTORIAL How to talk on the phone

Andrew: Hi, here are Andrew and Emily from *Channel Cool!* again. Do you remember? The last time we talked about finding a cheap place to stay. Today, we want to show you how you talk to your host on the phone.

Emily: I'm sure many people are nervous about that!

Andrew: They don't need to be nervous. Let's show them how to do it!

Emily: Can I be the host?

Andrew: Ok, Emily. You're the host. Her name is Mary.

Emily: Hello?

Andrew: Hello, this is Andrew Young. Can I speak to Mary, please?

Emily: Hi, Andrew. This is Mary. How are you?

Andrew: I'm fine, thanks. How are you?

Emily: Great thanks. What can I do for you?

Andrew: I'm calling about your offer of a sofa. Is the sofa available from 10 to 13 April?

Emily: Sorry, can you repeat the dates again, please? I didn't understand you.

Andrew: Sure! From 10 to 13 April.

Emily: That's fine. You can have the bed in our spare room.

Andrew: Well, that sounds great. It's my first time in Dublin. Can you recommend any interesting events?

Emily: Of course, Dublin is a great city for live music. You can listen to bands in almost every pub at the weekend.

Andrew: I love live music. I'm arriving at Dublin Airport on 10 April at 5 in the afternoon. How do I get to your place?

Emily: Well, take the number 747 bus from the airport into the city. Then you get off at the last stop. You need to get a number 51. Ask the driver to drop you off at McHenry Street. The flat is number 34A.

Andrew: Great, thank you very much. I'm looking forward to meeting you.

Emily: Ok, Andrew, see you soon. Take care, bye.

Andrew: Bye.

Emily: So guys, now you know how to make a phone call. Easy, right? Join us again soon on *Channel Cool!*

Unit 4

A 27 2 Listening: Let me tell you about my job!

Working is stressful and boring? Not if you have the right job! Mike, Anna und Tom will tell you about their jobs and what they like about it. You will also find out which qualities they need!

Mike: Hi, my name's Mike. I like being outside all the time. And not only when the sun is shining, but also when it's windy or raining. I can't imagine sitting in an office all day long. That's why I like being a gardener. Sometimes I have to work hard, but at the end of the day when the work is done, it's great to see how beautiful everything is. I like working with my hands but I'm also good at using machines like mowers.

Anna: Hey, I'm Anna and I love spending time with children. My dream job is to work as a nursery school teacher. The most important thing in this job is to be patient with the children. And I think you also have to be a caring person. I enjoy playing games with the kids and we laugh a lot. Sometimes I have to comfort the kids when they're sick or have hurt themselves.

Tom: Hello, I'm Tom. I work as a cook in a restaurant. I love working with food because you can be very creative. Of course you also need to be quick and hard-working, especially at the weekends when we have many guests. And you need to be able to work in a team. There are nine people working together in our kitchen.

A 33 3 TUTORIAL Making arrangements on the phone

Andrew: Hi, this is Andrew again for *Channel Cool!*. Today we want to show you how to make arrangements on the phone. I've found a summer job in Sweden and my new boss Sofia phones me. I will do a role play with Rebecca – she's my boss Sofia.

Rebecca: That's right. I'm Sofia from *Swedish Tourism*.

Andrew: Hello, Andrew Young speaking.

Rebecca: Hi Andrew. This is Sofia at *Swedish Tourism*. We really liked your application. Are you still interested in the job?

Andrew: Yes, of course. That's fantastic!

Rebecca: We need people between June and September. When will you come to Sweden?

Andrew: I'll have time in July. Will four weeks be ok?
Rebecca: Oh yes. Will you fly to Stockholm?
Andrew: Yes, I think so. How will I get to the island?
Rebecca: We have a small bus and we'll collect you from the airport. Will you send me an e-mail with your flight details?
Andrew: Oh sure, I can do that. What will I need to bring? Will I need a sleeping bag?
Rebecca: Yes, you will. You'll also need working clothes when you clean the beach. And bring a lot of sun cream and a hat. It will be sunny on the island in July.
Andrew: Really? That's great. How many helpers will be in the team?
Rebecca: We will have four teams on the island. Each team will work at a different location: on the beach or in the forest or at information centres. I think that you'll be a good guy to have on the beach.
Andrew: Oh, I hope so!
Rebecca: I'm looking forward to meeting you in July.
Andrew: Me too. See you then. Goodbye.
Rebecca: Goodbye.
Andrew: Well, now you know how to make a phone call. And you can make arrangements with somebody. See you soon on *Channel Cool!*

Unit 5

A 38

2 Listening: A podcast by a trainee team assistant

Jenny: Hi, my name's Jenny Sievers and I'm 18 years old. I'm training to be a team assistant at *GoGlobal Fairs* in Essen in Germany. I have been with *GoGlobal* for six months and I've already learned a lot about how to organize events. Why did I choose event organization? Well, when I finished school last summer, I got a job as a helper at the exhibition hall in Essen. And that was it! I so enjoyed the busy atmosphere at the trade fairs and I loved meeting people from all over the world. I thought that working at trade fairs was exactly my kind of job.
I talked to an agent at my local employment office. He gave me the addresses of companies that organize events. I checked *GoGlobal Fairs*' website for job adverts and saw that they actually wanted people. Before I applied for the job at *GoGlobal Fairs* I sat down with my best friend. We read the advert again. She helped me to make a list of the skills that I needed for the job. My work experience at the exhibition hall and the list of skills looked good in my CV, I can tell you. *GoGlobal Fairs* only wanted online applications and CVs in English. The company works with lots of foreign partners and customers, and English is the language that everyone speaks.
I did a phone interview with *GoGlobal Fairs*. I was really nervous before the interview. But I was really lucky – I got the job!

A 45

Test yourself: Aufgabe b), c)

Jenny: *Hallo, Jenny Sievers.*
Mr Malone: Hello, is that Jenny? This is Mark Malone at *GoGlobal Fairs*.
Jenny: Oh hello, Mr Malone. Yes, it's me Jenny Sievers.
Mr Malone: Ok Jenny, I'm calling to do a phone interview with you. Are you free at the moment?
Jenny: Yes, of course I am.
Mr Malone: Great, let's start. First, could you tell me what you are doing at the moment?
Jenny: Certainly. I'm doing a one-year business course at a vocational college here in Germany. I'll finish my course in June this year.
Mr Malone: Thank you, Jenny. Why do you want to work for us?
Jenny: I've checked your website and I think *GoGlobal Fairs* is a really interesting company to work for. You organize events around the world and you offer a good training programme.
Mr Malone: Ok. Can you tell me about your work experience?
Jenny: Well, this year I have worked in the exhibition hall in Essen. I worked in the café for special guests. We also brought drinks and snacks to the stands. We worked in teams of four or five people. I really liked working in a team and meeting people from all over the world.
Mr Malone: Ok, Jenny. This will be my last question. Why should we give you the job?
Jenny: Well, I am very well organized. I think that is necessary when you organize events. I'm good at languages and I don't mind working long hours. I think that happens a lot when you work at events.
Mr Malone: That's true. Do you have any questions for me, Jenny?
Jenny: Yes, I do. When does the job start? There wasn't a date in the job advert.
Mr Malone: We want the person to start in August.
Jenny: Oh great. That suits me very well. Thank you Mr Malone.
Mr Malone: We are doing a number of interviews at the moment. We will contact you as soon as we have decided who we want for the position. I think that will be in two weeks. Is that ok with you?
Jenny: Yes of course, Mr Malone.
Mr Malone: It was nice talking to you Jenny.
Jenny: Thank you for giving me the interview, Mr Malone. I look forward to hearing from you.
Mr Malone: Goodbye Jenny.
Jenny: Goodbye.

Unit 6

A 46 2 Listening: At a hotel

Lara: *Guten Tag, kann ich Ihnen helfen?*
Mr Johansson: Hello, my name is Johansson. I've booked a room for three people. That's for me, my wife and small son.
Lara: Welcome to Munich, Mr Johansson. I hope you had a good journey.
Mr Johansson: No, we didn't. Our plane from Sweden was two hours late. And our taxi got stuck in traffic for 40 minutes.
Lara: I'm sorry to hear that. Traffic is often bad on Fridays. So Mr Johansson, I see you've booked a double room for three nights.
Mr Johansson: Yes, a double room with a child's bed.
Lara: Let me have a look. An extra bed ... We don't have any information about a child's bed.
Mr Johansson: That can't be right. Look, this is the e-mail confirmation from your hotel. It says a double room with a double bed and a bed for a child.
Lara: Oh dear, you're right. We'll bring up a child's bed immediately. Oh, I'm afraid that your room isn't ready yet. Maybe you could wait in the lounge ...
Mrs Johansson: Ole, I don't want to wait in the lounge. It's 1 o'clock and Arvid is tired and ...
Lara: Of course, Mrs Johansson, I understand. Perhaps I can give you a different room. Yes room 429 is ready. It has a nice view of the park.
Mr Johansson: Ok, thank you.
Lara: Yes, it's a very nice room with a balcony. Here's your key. Your room is on the fourth floor. I'll call the porter to help you with the bags.
Mr Johansson: Thanks.
Lara: You're welcome, Mr Johansson!

A 48 1 TUTORIAL Talking about plans

Emily: Good morning everyone, this is Emily from *Channel Cool!* Today we're going to talk about plans for the future and what people are going to do after school. I'm going to interview some students for *Channel Cool!* And my question is: What are your plans for the future?
Benjamin: I'm going to visit my aunt and uncle in Australia after school. They have a hotel and I'm going to work there for two months. I'm not going to get much pay. The hotel's near the beach so I'm going to learn to surf in the afternoons.
Rebecca: I'm going to start an apprenticeship with a big catering company in London. I'm going to move into a shared flat and I'm very excited to meet my new flatmates.
Andrew: Well most of my friends are going to look for jobs but I'm going to stay at college and do a business course. Before the next school year starts I'm going to travel through Spain.
Emily: As you can see, it's going to be an exciting time for many of you. Now you know how to talk about your plans for the future! This is Emily for *Channel Cool!*, thanks for listening!

A 54 Test yourself: Aufgabe d), e)

Mr Blair: Good morning, Sven. You're early again today. That's good.
Sven: Hello Mr Blair. That's right. I don't like to come in late and be stressed for the rest of the day.
Mr Blair: Of course. Are you enjoying your time here Sven?
Sven: Yes I am. It's different to what I expected but I'm learning a lot.
Mr Blair: Good. We're very happy with your work here, too. You are well organized and you work well in the team. Do you remember what I said yesterday, you know, about being too direct with customers?
Sven: Yes Mr Blair. I will try to be more polite to customers. In Germany we don't say "sorry" or "you're right" as often as English people do.
Mr Blair: I see. I think, Sven, that you're good at finding answers to problems. Here in England, when you say "I'm sorry" that is the first part of the answer. It means you can see the customer's problem. Then the customer can listen more to the rest of the answer.
Sven: Thank you for explaining, Mr Blair.
Mr Blair: No problem. By the way I noticed that you don't understand Matt's jokes. Don't worry! Nobody in the team understands his jokes!
Sven: Well I'm happy to hear that.

6.1 Getty Images Plus (PeopleImages), München; **6.2** dreamstime.com (Yulia Grigoryeva), Brentwood, TN; **6.3** Getty Images Plus (PeopleImages), München; **6.4** iStockphoto (AmyLaughinghouse), Calgary, Alberta; **6.5** iStockphoto (becon), Calgary, Alberta; **6.6** iStockphoto (valentinrussanov), Calgary, Alberta; **8.1** iStockphoto (ollo), Calgary, Alberta; **8.2** shutterstock (Jag_cz), New York, NY; **8.3** Getty Images (Gary Wolstenholme, Collection: Redferns), München; **8.4** Getty Images (Tim Mosenfelder), München; **10.1-4** Franconia Films (Moritz Weiß), Selb; **11.1** iStockphoto (pidjoe), Calgary, Alberta; **11.2** shutterstock (Monkey Business Images), New York, NY; **11.3** Getty Images Plus (mediaphotos), München; **11.4** iStockphoto (martinedoucet), Calgary, Alberta; **11.5** iStockphoto (tomazl), Calgary, Alberta; **11.6** Getty Images (Paul Bradbury, Collection: OJO Images), München; **11.7** plainpicture GmbH & Co. KG (beyond/Oscar Abrahams), Hamburg; **11.8** Getty Images Plus (vitranc), München; **12.1** Getty Images Plus (sturti), München; **12.2** shutterstock (CandyBox Images), New York, NY; **12.3** Getty Images (Science Photo Library - IAN HOOTON., Collection: Brand X Pictures), München; **13.1** iStockphoto (Antonio_Diaz), Calgary, Alberta; **13.2** iStockphoto (Antonio_Diaz), Calgary, Alberta; **13.3** iStockphoto (Antonio_Diaz), Calgary, Alberta; **13.4** Getty Images (Westend61), München; **15** plainpicture GmbH & Co. KG (Franke + Mans), Hamburg; **16.1** Getty Images Plus (mediaphotos), München; **16.2** iStockphoto (pidjoe), Calgary, Alberta; **16.3** shutterstock (Monkey Business Images), New York, NY; **16.4** iStockphoto (martinedoucet), Calgary, Alberta; **18.1** shutterstock (vvoe), New York, NY; **18.2** Getty Images Plus (izusek), München; **18.3** Klett-Archiv (Weissmann, Moskau); **18.4** plainpicture GmbH & Co. KG (Maskot), Hamburg; **18.5** Getty Images Plus (SolStock), München; **18.6** plainpicture GmbH & Co. KG (Westend61/Joseffson), Hamburg; **19** Getty Images (Peter Muller, Collection: Cultura), München; **20.1** Getty Images Plus (KatarzynaBialasiewicz), München; **20.2** shutterstock (hecke61), New York, NY; **20.3** Getty Images Plus (domin_domin), München; **22.1-2**; **23.1-3** Franconia Films (Moritz Weiß), Selb; **26.1** Getty Images Plus (kali9), München; **26.2** shutterstock (Kot500), New York, NY; **26.3** shutterstock (Kot500), New York, NY; **26.4** Getty Images Plus (Lizalica), München; **26.5** shutterstock (Dragon Images), New York, NY; **26.6** shutterstock (Dragon Images), New York, NY; **27.1** Adobe Stock (Andrey Popov), Dublin; **27.2** Adobe Stock (Andrey Popov), Dublin; **27.3** Adobe Stock (Andrey Popov), Dublin; **29.1** Getty Images Plus (AntonioGuillem), München; **29.2** Getty Images Plus (nd3000), München; **29.3** Getty Images Plus (AndreyPopov), München; **30** Adobe Stock (okorokovanatalya), Dublin; **32.1** Getty Images (Paul Bradbury, Collection: OJO Images), München; **32.2** Getty Images Plus (Hinterhaus Productions), München; **32.2** Getty Images Plus (vgajic), München; **32.3** plainpicture GmbH & Co. KG (Phillip Gätz), Hamburg; **32.4** Getty Images Plus (Klaus Vedfelt), München; **32.5** Getty Images (Adie Bush, Collection: Cultura), München; **32.6** Getty Images Plus (Hinterhaus Productions), München; **32.7** plainpicture GmbH & Co. KG (Franco Cozzo), Hamburg; **34.1** Getty Images (Adie Bush, Collection: Cultura), München; **34.2** Getty Images Plus (Hinterhaus Productions), München; **34.3** Getty Images Plus (vgajic), München; **36** Franconia Films (Moritz Weiß), Selb; **37.1** Getty Images Plus (levers2007), München; **37.2** Getty Images Plus (Shootdiem), München; **37.3** iStockphoto (LightFieldStudios), Calgary, Alberta; **37.4-5**; **39.1-2** Franconia Films (Moritz Weiß), Selb; **40.1** Getty Images Plus (electravk), München; **40.2** Getty Images Plus (andresr), München; **40.3** PantherMedia GmbH (Creatista), München; **41.1** Getty Images Plus (TommL), München; **41.2** Picture-Alliance (Martin Schutt), Frankfurt; **41.3** Getty Images RF (Photodisc), München; **41.4** Getty Images Plus (hillaryfox), München; **45** Getty Images Plus (mastapiece), München; **46.1** Getty Images Plus (izusek), München; **46.2** shutterstock (Syda Productions), New York, NY; **46.3** Getty Images (Westend61), München; **46.4** Getty Images Plus (fotoedu), München; **46.5** shutterstock (Photo Oz), New York, NY; **46.6** Getty Images Plus (FatCamera), München; **50** Getty Images Plus (keiichihiki), München; **51.1** Getty Images Plus (phototiger), München; **51.2**; **52.1-2**; **53** Franconia Films (Moritz Weiß, Marktredwitz), Selb; **54.1** Getty Images Plus (jacoblund), München; **54.2** Getty Images Plus (Portra), München; **54.3** Getty Images Plus (Chalffy), München; **55.1** Getty Images Plus (Imgorthand), München; **55.2** Getty Images Plus (Vesnaandjic), München; **60.1** Getty Images Plus (fizkes), München; **60.2** Getty Images Plus (PeopleImages), München; **60.3** VISUM Foto GmbH (Thomas Langreder), Hannover; **60.4** Getty Images Plus (grinvalds), München; **60.5** Getty Images Plus (Katerina Sisperova), München; **62** Adobe Stock (conorcrowe), Dublin; **64.1-4**; **65.1-2** Franconia Films (Moritz Weiß), Selb; **66.1** Adobe Stock (giorgiomtb), Dublin; **66.2** Getty Images Plus (Sjale), München; **66.3** Getty Images Plus (dimid_86), München; **66.4** Getty Images Plus (igor_kell), München; **72.1** Getty Images Plus (moonboard), München; **72.2** Getty Images Plus (JGI/Jamie Grill), München; **72.3** Adobe Stock (Production Perig), Dublin; **72.4** Getty Images (Paul Bradbury, Collection: OJO Images), München; **72.5** Getty Images Plus (PeopleImages), München; **72.6** Getty Images (Fuse, Collection: Corbis), München; **74** Getty Images Plus (andresr), München; **76**; **77.1-2** Franconia Films (Moritz Weiß, Marktredwitz), Selb; **78.1** Alamy stock photo (Jeff Gilbert), Abingdon, Oxon; **78.2** Getty Images Plus (shironosov), München; **79** iStockphoto (PeopleImages), Calgary, Alberta, **Umschlagbild** Getty Images RF (estend61), München.

Sollte es in einem Einzelfall nicht gelungen sein, den korrekten Rechteinhaber ausfindig zu machen, so werden berechtigte Ansprüche selbstverständlich im Rahmen der üblichen Regelungen abgegolten.

Differenziert unterrichten!
Keep Cool! kann parallel zu Cool! im Unterricht eingesetzt werden.
Ziel: Niveau A1

Berufsvorbereitung Englisch

Keep Cool!

Lehrerausgabe mit Video-DVD

Teildruck
Ohne Video-DVD
Die Verkaufsauflage erscheint unter der ISBN 978-3-12-808126-7

Klett

Contents

1 Making new friends

im392p

A

B

C

D

E

F

1 At a festival

a) *Kreuzen Sie an, was auf den Bildern zu sehen ist.*

- [X] a big stage
- [X] a singer
- [X] wellingtons
- [X] a festival
- [ ] great music
- [X] fans
- [ ] a food truck menu
- [X] a camping site
- [X] wristbands
- [X] mud
- [X] hamburgers
- [ ] security
- [ ] tickets
- [X] sunglasses
- [X] tents

Am Ende der Unit kann ich ...

- [ ] sagen, wie ich heiße.
- [ ] sagen, wo ich wohne.
- [ ] Menschen fragen, wie sie heißen und wo sie wohnen.

b) *Ordnen Sie die Begriffe aus Aufgabe a) den Fotos zu ⇄.*

Photo A *a singer*
Photo B *fans, sunglasses, a festival, wristbands*
Photo C *a camping site, tents*
Photo D *wellingtons, mud*
Photo E *wristbands, a big stage*
Photo F *hamburgers*

c) *Zu welchem Foto passt diese Beschreibung?* → S 1

I can see many people. They are at a festival. Some of them are wearing wristbands.

You say ...
I can see a food truck.
There is a stage ...
There are many tents ...

Die Beschreibung passt zu Foto *B*.

2 Listening: At the Hurricane festival → S 7 → Information

A 1

a) *Unterstreichen Sie die richtigen Aussagen.*

1. Das Hurricane-Festival findet in Süddeutschland / Norddeutschland / Ostdeutschland statt.
2. Das Festival dauert zwei Tage / drei Tage / eine Woche.
3. Es ist ein Heavy-Metal-Festival / Reggae-Festival / Rockfestival.
4. Sie können im Zelt / in der Jugendherberge / bei Gastfamilien übernachten.

b) *Welcher Satz ist richtig? Unterstreichen Sie.*

1. The festival lasts two days / three days / seven days.
2. There are about 100 bands / 200 bands / 1,000 bands.
3. The tickets cost from 80 to 180 euros / 180 to 515 euros / 180 to 550 euros.
4. More than 7,000 fans / 17,000 fans / 70,000 fans come to see the bands.
5. The cleaners look after 1,700 toilets / 1,800 toilets / 1,900 toilets.

3 Your turn

a) *Was ist an Musikfestivals schön? Was ist nicht so schön? Ordnen Sie die Begriffe zu.*

great music | food trucks | mud | loud | young people | expensive | party

👍	👎
Individuelle Lösung	

b) *Welcher Aussage stimmen Sie zu? Kreuzen Sie an.*

- [ ] I like music festivals! You can enjoy great music and see many bands.
- [ ] I don't like music festivals! They are loud and expensive. Sometimes there is a lot of mud.

4 Reading: Amazing facts about festivals → S2

A2

Es gibt seit über 3000 Jahren Musikfestivals! Manche sind sogar unter Wasser oder an Silvester. Das berühmteste Festival ist in Glastonbury, England.

BLOG

A

B

C

D

Music festivals

The tradition of music festivals is very old. The first music festivals took place 3,000 years ago in Greece. Let's look at some amazing festivals today.

1. The deepest festival is under the sea. It is called the Lower Keys Underwater Festival in Florida. Divers can listen to music and watch tropical fish.
2. The coldest music festival is the Snow Globe Festival in California. On New Year's Eve, you can listen and dance to bands in the snow.
3. The most famous festival in England is probably Glastonbury Festival. Almost 50 years ago, the tickets were only £1 and you even got a glass of fresh milk for free. Glastonbury Festival is great fun but don't forget to bring a good raincoat!

5 **diver** *Taucher/-in;* **tropical** *tropisch* – 6 **New Year's Eve** *Silvester* – 8 **probably** *wahrscheinlich* – 9 **even** *sogar*

a) *Ordnen Sie die Texte 1.–3. den passenden Bildern zu ⇄. Welches Bild passt nicht dazu?*

Text 1 goes with picture B. - Text 2: D - Text 3: C

Bild A passt nicht

b) *Kreuzen Sie das richtige Kästchen an ✗: richtig* (true) *oder falsch* (false)*?* → **Information**

	true	false
1. The first music festivals in history were in Canada.	☐	X
2. The Lower Keys Festival is under the sea.	X	☐
3. You can go to the Snow Globe Festival in California after Christmas.	X	☐
4. Fans get a raincoat for free with the ticket to Glastonbury Festival.	☐	X

c) *Beantworten Sie die Fragen auf Deutsch. Die Zeilenangaben helfen Ihnen.*

1. Wann fanden die ersten Musikfestivals statt (Z. 2)? Vor 3.000 Jahren.
2. Auf welchem Festival wird man auf jeden Fall nass (Z. 4)? Glastonbury Festival.
3. Was gab es früher beim Glastonbury Festival umsonst (Z. 9)? Ein Glas Milch.

5 Getting around a festival

a) *Ordnen Sie die Bilder den richtigen Begriffen zu ⇄.*

cash machine | toilets | police | food truck | recharge tent | ~~paramedics~~ | information

1. paramedics
2. information
3. toilets
4. food truck
5. recharge tent
6. cash machine
7. police

b) *Sie arbeiten an der Information eines Musikfestivals. Beantworten Sie die Fragen.*

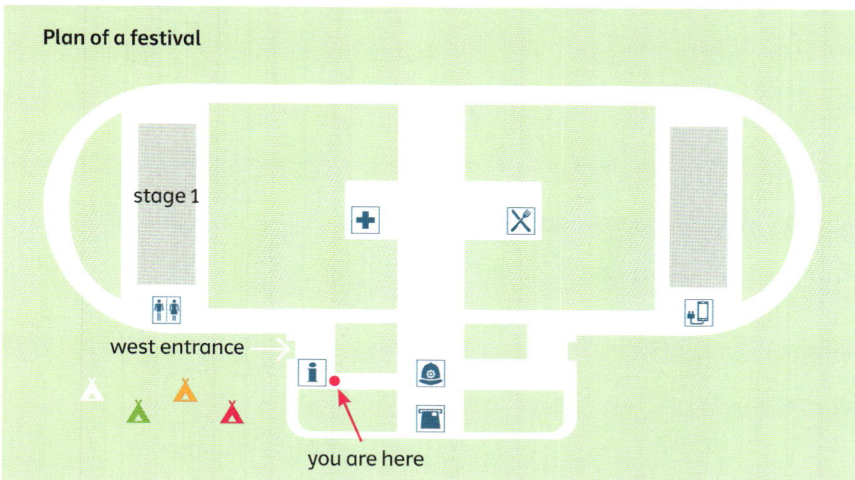

You say ...

- turn left ←
- turn right →
- walk straight on ↑
- next to
- opposite → ←
- behind
- in front of

1. "Excuse me, where are the toilets?"

   You: *Turn left here and walk straight on. The toilets are in front of you.*

2. "I need some cash. Is there a cash machine near here?"

   You: *Yes, walk straight on. Then turn right at the police tent.*

3. "I've hurt my leg. Can you tell me the way to the paramedics, please?"

   You: *Of course. Walk straight on and turn left at the police tent. The paramedics are opposite stage 1.*

4. "My smartphone is dead. Can you help me?"

   You: *Sure. Walk straight on, then turn left at the east entrance. Turn right and the recharge tent is in front of you.*

c) *Wählen Sie eine der Situationen in b) aus. Spielen Sie sie mit einem Partner/einer Partnerin nach.*

ODER

- *Überlegen Sie sich eine andere Situation an der Information. Spielen Sie sie mit einem Partner/einer Partnerin nach.*

Your task

Jugendliche aus aller Welt treffen sich auf einem Festival. Die gemeinsame Sprache ist Englisch.

Sie möchten andere Jugendliche kennenlernen. Kein Problem!
Rebecca, Andrew, Benjamin und Emily zeigen Ihnen, wie man das auf Englisch macht.

Meet the experts → S 3

1 TUTORIAL Getting to know people → G2

V1 A3

Hi, I'm Emily.
What's your name?

My name's Andrew.
Nice to meet you, Emily!

I'm Benjamin. I come from Brisbane in Australia.

My name is Rebecca.
Where are you from?

a) *Vervollständigen Sie die Sätze mit Ihren eigenen Angaben.*

Beispiel: I'm Mike. I come from Essen in Germany.

I'm ______________________. I come from ____________________ in ______________________.

b) *Fragen Sie einen Partner/eine Partnerin.*

1. What's your name?
2. Where are you from?

You say ...
1. What's your name?
2. Where are you from?

2 TUTORIAL Talking about yourself → G1

V2 A4

a) *Wer hat welches Hobby? Kreuzen Sie an.*

activities	Andrew	Emily	Benjamin	Rebecca
1. listening to hard rock		X		
2. sports			X	
3. shopping		X		X
4. hanging out with friends				X
5. free climbing			X	
6. listening to heavy metal	X			

b) *Vervollständigen Sie die Sätze.*

1. Andrew likes ☺ listening to heavy metal.
2. Emily doesn't like ☹ listening to heavy metal.
3. Benjamin loves ☺ sport but he doesn't like ☹ music.
4. Rebecca loves ☺ shopping and hanging out with friends.

V3 A5

3 TUTORIAL Talking about jobs

a) *Über welche Jobs spricht Emily? Kreuzen Sie die richtigen Kästchen an.*

[X] car mechanic

[X] shop assistant

[X] hairdresser

[ ] caterer

[ ] personal assistant

[ ] security

[X] waitress/waiter

[X] electrician

b) *Was sagt Emily über die folgenden Jobs? Kreuzen Sie die richtige Antwort an.*

1. A car mechanic …
   - [X] repairs engines.
   - [ ] checks broken parts.
   - [ ] likes working with people.

2. A hairdresser's main tasks are …
   - [ ] chatting to other hairdressers.
   - [X] cutting hair.
   - [ ] making coffee.

3. An electrician …
   - [ ] repairs engines.
   - [X] works in people's homes.
   - [ ] chats to customers.

4. A waiter's main tasks are …
   - [X] taking orders.
   - [ ] cleaning the kitchen.
   - [ ] meeting people.

● c) *Wählen Sie einen der Jobs in Aufgabe b).*
Nennen Sie einem Partner/einer Partnerin auf Englisch drei Dinge, die man in diesem Job tut.

Example: A waiter serves food.

Individuelle Lösung

A6

1 Paramedic: Emma's blog → S 2

Emma erzählt Ihnen etwas über ihren Beruf als Sanitäterin: welche Aufgaben sie hat, wo sie arbeitet und welche Voraussetzungen für den Job wichtig sind.

BLOG

A

B

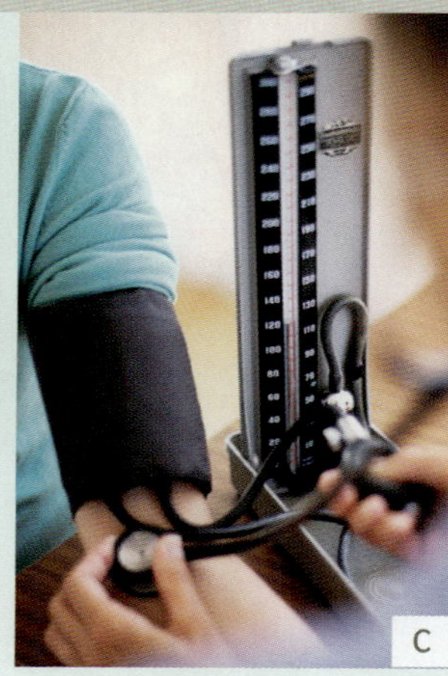

C

Hello, I'm Emma. I'm a paramedic and I normally work in a hospital. I meet many people from all over the world every day. I like helping people and making them feel better. Some people are afraid because they are sick. So I have to be calm and friendly.

Do you want to know what I do every day? Well, I check people's blood pressure, give injections and work with the doctor. I sometimes have to go out in an ambulance, for example when there is a big accident in a factory. We also help when there is a road accident, for example when a person falls off his or her bike.

Paramedics like me also go to events like festivals and football matches in case somebody gets hurt. That's why I sometimes work at weekends or at night.

I really love my job! It can be sad or exciting or tiring but it's different every day.

3 **afraid** *ängstlich*; **sick** *krank*; **calm** *ruhig* – 4 **blood pressure** *Blutdruck* – 5 **injection** *Spritze* – 6 **accident** *Unfall*; **factory** *Fabrik* – 8 **in case** *falls* – 10 **tiring** *ermüdend*; **different** *anders*

a) *Was ist spannend an diesem Job? Unterstreichen Sie im Text mit blau.*

b) *Was ist schwierig an diesem Job? Unterstreichen Sie im Text mit rot.*

c) *Was sagt Emma über die Bilder? Finden Sie die Stelle im Text. Die Zeilenangaben helfen Ihnen.*

Photo A (Z. 5) *I sometimes have to go out in an ambulance.*

Photo B (Z. 6) *We also help when there is a road accident, for example when a person falls off his or her bike.*

Photo C (Z. 4) *I check people's blood pressure.*

d) *Welche Eigenschaften braucht man als Sanitäter? Vervollständigen Sie die Sätze.*

1. A paramedic must be *calm* and *friendly*.
2. A paramedic likes *helping people* and *making them feel better*.

e) *Miriam sagt: „Dieser Beruf ist nichts für mich. Da muss man jeden Tag dasselbe tun. Das ist langweilig." Hat sie recht? Begründen Sie. Die unterstrichenen Textstellen aus a) und b) helfen Ihnen dabei.*

Individuelle Lösung

A7

2 Caterer: Looking for help

Hier sehen Sie eine Stellenanzeige. Ein Imbisswagen in Großbritannien sucht neue Mitarbeiter.

The Food Truck is looking for help for the summer.

Do you like meeting people at festivals and sports events?
Do you enjoy working in a small team?
Do you like doing different tasks every day?
Do you hate wearing a uniform?
Do you like travelling?

Then **The Food Truck** wants to hear from you.

We cook and serve Asian and Irish food all over Ireland.
The working hours are from 11 a.m. to 9 p.m.
The day starts at the vegetable market.
Cooking begins at 12 o' clock.
We have to clean the truck by 9 p.m.

Interested?
Then contact Charlie from **The Food Truck** at food@truck.

serving food

cooking

cleaning

taking money

8 **to enjoy** *genießen* – 13 **to serve** *servieren*; **Asian** *asiatisch*

a) *Sagen Sie einem Partner/einer Partnerin etwas über den Job.*
Example: You start work at 11 o' clock.

b) *Welche Seiten des Jobs gefallen Ihnen? Unterstreichen Sie mit blau.*
Welche Seiten des Jobs gefallen Ihnen nicht? Unterstreichen Sie mit rot.

● **c)** *Sagen Sie Ihrem Partner/Ihrer Partnerin auf Englisch, ob der Job für Sie interessant ist oder nicht.*
Nutzen Sie Ihre unterstrichenen Stellen im Text.

Example: You do different tasks every day.

You say ...
I like the job because ...
I don't like the job because ...

Individuelle Lösung

1 Festivals

a) *Vervollständigen Sie das Wortnetz. Verwenden Sie die Wörter aus den Kästchen.* → S 4

band | cash machine | drums | entrance | tents | hamburger | menu | music | food truck | recharge tent | toilets | wellingtons | wristband

- festivals
  - plan
    - *cash machine*
    - *entrance*
    - *recharge tent*
    - *toilets*
  - stages
    - *band*
    - *music*
    - *drums*
  - fans
    - *wristband*
    - *tents*
    - *wellingtons*
  - food
    - *menu*
    - *food truck*
    - *hamburger*

b) *Verbinden* ⇄ *Sie die Satzanfänge mit den richtigen Satzenden.*

1. The event lasts
2. The festival takes place
3. The ticket costs
4. We can put up
5. You can party all day
6. Everyone enjoys

a) 30 pounds.
b) a tent.
c) three days.
d) the great music.
e) in the north of Germany.
f) with your friends.

(Lösung: 1 – c, 2 – e, 3 – a, 4 – b, 5 – f, 6 – d)

2 Giving directions

a) *Vervollständigen Sie die Sätze.*

1. Sie möchten sagen, dass man am Imbisswagen links gehen soll.
   "Turn *left at the food truck.*"
2. Sie möchten sagen, dass die Sanitäter gegenüber vom Westeingang sind.
   "The paramedics are *opposite the west entrance.*"
3. Sie möchten sagen, dass man hinter der Bühne rechts gehen soll.
   "Turn *right behind the stage.*"
4. Sie möchten sagen, dass die Polizei vor dem Geldautomaten ist.
   "The police are *in front of the cash machine.*"

Your turn

Sie sind auf einem Festival und möchten andere Jugendliche kennenlernen. Sie möchten sich vorstellen. Tipp: Schauen Sie sich noch einmal die Tutorials an, um wichtige Redewendungen zu lernen.

Partner B

Partner A

Schritt 1:

Schauen Sie sich die Notizzettel von Tom und Sarah an.

Tom

- 20 years old
- London
- soccer, drums
- favourite country: Australia
- dream job: electrician

Sarah

- 19 years old
- Brentford
- shopping, swimming
- dream job: sales assistant

Schritt 2:

Machen Sie sich einen eigenen Notizzettel.

name | … years old | come from … | free time: … | like … | don't like …

Schritt 3:

Finden Sie in der Klasse einen Partner/eine Partnerin und stellen Sie sich gegenseitig vor. Üben Sie den Dialog mehrfach ein. Um Ihren Dialog realistischer zu machen, können Sie die Wörter / Sätze im „You say-Kasten" verwenden.

You say …

Well, … / Oh really? /
That's interesting.
What about you? / Wow! / Oh no …

Schritt 4:

Spielen Sie den Dialog einem anderen Pärchen vor.

A8

Mit Zahlen umgehen

Denken Sie kurz darüber nach, in welchen Situationen Sie jeden Tag Zahlen sehen oder benutzen … Zum Beispiel, wenn Sie auf den Kalender schauen, die Uhrzeit lesen, einkaufen, eine Hausnummer suchen oder auf den Fahrplan schauen.

Emily und Andrew unterhalten sich über das *Rock in May Festival*, das sie bereits letztes Jahr besucht haben.

Emily: Hey, let's go to *Rock in May*!
Andrew: Yes, it's always great fun. Look, it's on 3 May.
Emily: Oh, that's in two days. Let's call the ticket hotline and book our tickets.
Andrew: Great idea. The number is …34418.
Emily: Oh look, the tickets are 35 pounds! And we also need to buy train tickets.
Andrew: That's a lot. But there is a special offer: tickets are 15 pounds when you only go to see the first bands in the morning.
Emily: When does the first band start?
Andrew: At 10 o'clock.
Emily: That's a good idea, let's do that!

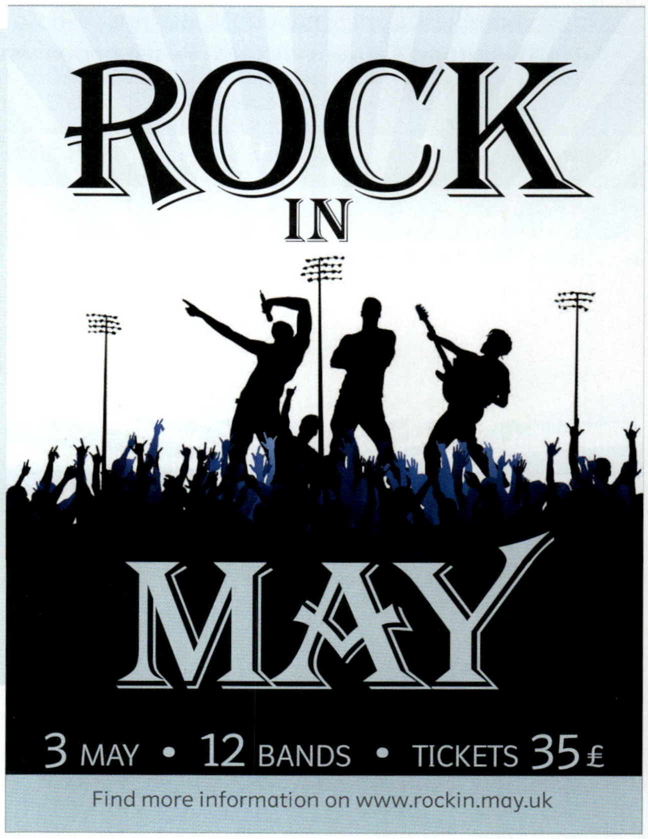

a) *Lesen Sie die Uhrzeiten vor. Eine Übersicht der englischen Zahlen und wichtigen Angaben für die Uhrzeit finden Sie am Ende des Buchs auf Seite 112.*

1. 02:00 2. 13:45 3. 17:10 4. 09:25 5. 12:30 6. 05:37

You say …

Im Alltag sagt man meistens nur "let's meet at 5" – aus der Situation geht hervor, ob 5 Uhr morgens oder 17 Uhr nachmittags gemeint ist. Am Flughafen oder auf Fahrplänen lesen Sie oft: 5 a.m. (= 5 Uhr morgens) bzw. 5 p.m. (= 17 Uhr abends).

b) *Arbeiten Sie mit einem Partner/einer Partnerin. Fragen Sie sich gegenseitig nach Ihrer Telefonnummer.*

Beispiel:
A: What's your phone number?
B: My number is …

c) *Arbeiten Sie mit einem Partner/einer Partnerin. Lesen Sie sich gegenseitig die Telefonnummern vor. Finden Sie heraus, zu welchem Land die Nummern gehören.*

1. 0049 30 8827 2. 01 555 739 3. 0039 38 9912 4. 0098 729 482 4. 0046 829 419

1. The country is *Germany*
2. The country is *USA*
3. The country is *Italy*
4. The country is *Iran*
5. The country is *Sweden*

Culture Tip
Jedes Land hat seine eigene Vorwahl (z. B. Deutschland: 0049). Danach kommt die Vorwahl des Ortes (z. B. Berlin: 030). Erst danach kommt die eigentliche Telefonnummer.

d) *Sagen Sie einem Partner/einer Partnerin die Preise der Produkte.*

Beispiel:
A: How much is the skirt?
B: It's 49 €.
A: And how much are the shoes?
B: They are 79,95 €.

Culture Tip
Viele Länder haben eine eigene Währung: 10 Euro entsprechen z. B. umgerechnet ca. 8,80 britische Pfund oder 843 afghanische Afghani.

e) *Lesen Sie vor und sagen Sie, wie es weitergeht. Nennen Sie mindestens eine Zahl.*

1. 2 – 4 – 6 – 8 – . . . *(10 – 12)*
2. 10 – 20 – 30 – 40 – . . . *(50 – 60)*
3. 3 – 9 – 18 – 36 – . . . *(72 – 144)*
4. 36 – 30 – 24 – 18 – . . . *(12 – 6)*
5. 81 – 89 – 97 – 105 – . . . *(113 – 121)*

You say . . .
Im Englischen sagt man zuerst die Zehnerzahl, dann die Einerzahl: **twenty**-three. Im Deutschen ist es umgekehrt: dreiund**zwanzig**. Bei Telefonnummern wird jede Zahl einzeln diktiert, außer bei Doppellungen: 5534 = double five three four.

● **f)** *Lösen Sie die Rechenaufgaben, schreiben Sie die Zahlen dabei aus. Lesen Sie die Rechnungen und die Lösung anschließend laut einem Partner/einer Partnerin vor.*

1. 14 + 7 = *fourteen + seven = twenty-one*
2. 32 – 2 = *thirty-two – two = thirty*
3. 116 + 4 = *one hundred and sixteen + four = one hundred and twenty*
4. 81 – 11 = *eighty-one – eleven = seventy*
5. 1002 + 13 = *one thousand and two + thirteen = one thousand and fifteen*
6. 223 + 27 = *two hundred and twenty-three + twenty-seven = two hundred and fifty*

- Speziell für Schülerinnen und Schüler mit geringen Vorkenntnissen
- Passgenau zu Cool!: kann auch parallel im Unterricht eingesetzt werden
- Mit Tutorials, die Alltags- und Berufssituationen verständlich erklären
- Für jeden den passenden Zugang zur Sprache: Alle Tutorials stehen als Video- und Audio-Datei online kostenlos zur Verfügung
- Kommunikative Bewältigung von grundlegenden Alltagssituationen

Quellennachweis

Umschlag Getty Images RF (Westend61), München; **6.1** Getty Images Plus (PeopleImages), München; **6.2** dreamstime.com (Yulia Grigoryeva), Brentwood, TN; **6.3** Getty Images Plus (PeopleImages), München; **6.4** iStockphoto (AmyLaughinghouse), Calgary, Alberta; **6.5** iStockphoto (becon), Calgary, Alberta; **6.6** iStockphoto (valentinrussanov), Calgary, Alberta; **8.1** iStockphoto (ollo), Calgary, Alberta; **8.2** shutterstock (Jag_cz), New York, NY; **8.3** Getty Images (Gary Wolstenholme, Collection: Redferns), München; **8.4** Getty Images (Tim Mosenfelder), München; **10.1–4** Franconia Films (Moritz Weiß), Selb; **11.1** iStockphoto (pidjoe), Calgary, Alberta; **11.2** shutterstock (Monkey Business Images), New York, NY; **11.3** Getty Images Plus (mediaphotos), München; **11.4** iStockphoto (martinedoucet), Calgary, Alberta; **11.5** iStockphoto (tomazl), Calgary, Alberta; **11.6** Getty Images (Paul Bradbury, Collection: OJO Images), München; **11.7** plainpicture GmbH & Co. KG (beyond/Oscar Abrahams), Hamburg; **11.8** Getty Images Plus (vitranc), München; **12.1** Getty Images Plus (sturti), München; **12.2** shutterstock (CandyBox Images), New York, NY; **12.3** Getty Images (Science Photo Library - IAN HOOTON., Collection: Brand X Pictures), München; **13.1–3** iStockphoto (Antonio_Diaz), Calgary, Alberta; **13.4** Getty Images (Westend61), München; **15** plainpicture GmbH & Co. KG (Franke + Mans), Hamburg; **16** Getty Images Plus (nico_blue), München;

W 504164 (09/2018)

Ernst Klett Verlag GmbH
Postfach 10 26 45, 70022 Stuttgart
Telefon 0711 · 66 72 13 33, Telefax 0711 · 98 80 90 00 99
www.klett.de